Decolonizing Christianity

DECOLONIZING CHRISTIANITY

Becoming Badass Believers

Miguel A. De La Torre

WILLIAM B. EERDMANS PUBLISHING COMPANY
GRAND RAPIDS, MICHIGAN

Wm. B. Eerdmans Publishing Co.
4035 Park East Court SE, Grand Rapids, Michigan 49546
www.eerdmans.com

27 26 25 24 23 22 21   1 2 3 4 5 6 7

ISBN 978-0-8028-7847-2

Library of Congress Cataloging-in-Publication Data

Names: De La Torre, Miguel A., author.
Title: Decolonizing Christianity : becoming badass believers /
    Miguel A. De La Torre.
Description: Grand Rapids, Michigan : Wm. B. Eerdmans Publishing
    Company, [2021] | Includes bibliographical references. | Summary:
    "A call for American Christianity to stand in solidarity with mar-
    ginalized people and end its complicity with white supremacy"—
    Provided by publisher.
Identifiers: LCCN 2020040441 | ISBN 9780802878472
Subjects: LCSH: Christianity—United States. | Church work with
    minorities—United States. | Postcolonial theology.
Classification: LCC BR560 .D4 2021 | DDC 261.80973—dc23
LC record available at https://lccn.loc.gov/2020040441

Contents

1

Lest We Forget

The publication of *Burying White Privilege: Resurrecting a Badass Christianity* in late 2018 was controversial and made quite an impression on many people who identify as mainstream Christians. Several praised the book's candor and insight, offering constructive criticism. Perhaps the book was well received because the ideas it conveyed resonated with many who live on the margins as they attempt to survive what the legendary reggae musician Peter Tosh called the "shitstem." As could be expected, the book also met much condemnation, some of which was quite disparaging. Those choosing to hold white supremacy's feet to the fire can expect vicious ad hominem attacks. Character assassination and fallacious arguments concerning motive serve to distract readers from engaging with arguments made concerning the prevailing nationalist Christianity. True—some hated the book and demonized its author, while others, disagreeing with the author, nonetheless celebrated the opportunity for a conversation. There were also some white readers who, instead of wrestling with the text, chose the indulgence of using my words to self-flagellate. Wallowing in self-pity over their complicity with racist structures, some, to call attention to themselves, moaned more loudly than one would over a minor toothache, thus ignoring the pain being experienced by their others.

Seeking the Answer

One critique made by both defenders and detractors of the book became the main reason for writing this follow-up text. Among those who criticized *Burying White Privilege*, many discussed its failure to provide a remedy for Euro-Americans to implement, a solution to the overarching norm of white supremacy. "De La Torre does a tremendous job in diagnosing the disease," some wrote, "but he falls short in providing the treatment." These readers demanded concrete answers. Some pleaded, "Tell us what to do!" or asked, "What is the cure for what ails our racist society?" Some argued that while my disparaging comments concerning Eurocentric nationalist Christianity in general, and President Trump specifically, might have been therapeutic for some readers, they believed the book was unsuccessful because it lacked a plan of action that could bring repentance, healing, and salvation to whites. How dare the author diagnose the ailment without providing the antidote and end the book on such a note of hopelessness! they cried.

Imagine a spouse trapped in a physically abusive and violent relationship. Does one approach the domestically battered partner, whose lips are bleeding from being slapped, and demand that this person produce a thoughtful and measured solution for their physical and emotional maltreatment? And yet, in the cohabitation of different races and ethnicities that comprise our nation-house, those who are privileged and cloaked in the supremacism of whiteness expect those who have been physically exploited for centuries to administer the necessary balm to soothe their abusers' troubled souls. Can you see how offensive it is to ask those relegated to the margins of whiteness to provide the tonic that heals those who have dispossessed, disenfranchised, and disinherited them? Rather than dealing with their complicity, these whites are demanding that the sufferers provide the means to resolve their own suffering.

On the other side of this equation, even when solutions are continuously demanded from the abused, the answers they offer are ignored. Maybe the concerns of the battered are dismissed because they are voiced in anger or through too many tears of pain, making tormentors feel guilty or uncomfortable. Not only are the mistreated required to offer solutions, but they must present them in loving kindness and tender sensitivity lest aggressors feel threatened, misunderstood, offended, or aggravated. Regardless of how many times the marginalized have come forward to reason in good faith, they have been met with a refusal to listen. For this reason, the responsibility for dealing with spousal abuse ought to fall on the abuser and not the abused. Rather than focusing upon the ones being oppressed, we must keep the focus on their oppressors, holding the belligerent responsible. Constantly having to explain to members of the dominant culture how they have been exploitative while also providing remedies for one's own maltreatment takes a psychological toll on the marginalized. Those of us who encounter the daily micro- and at times macro-aggressions experience a cumulative emotional anguish that negatively impacts our mental and physical health. Many of us who have spent a lifetime having to tell these abusers how they should not be abusing us find ourselves wrestling—all too often—with self-doubt and self-loathing.

If the truth be told, white America already knows the answer. They know what needs to be done. And if they don't, they can simply Google it! Or better yet, read a book. Salvation, liberation, and redemption for the oppressed and the oppressor are not mysterious hidden secrets eluding humanity, only to be found by the chosen few. Justice does not rain down like living water nor righteousness flow like an everlasting stream because knowledge is absent and ignorance reigns. What is lacking, what has always been lacking, is will—the will to stop egregious cruelties that profit the exceptional few. The answer was articulated over two thousand years ago, but the powerful have accumulated so much earwax over the centuries that the good news is difficult for them to hear. But even when the privileged are able to hear the voices from their margins, complicity is still normalized by amnesia, more deafness, more blindness, and finally, unwillingness to believe what are the appropriate actions to take. Let the words of this book serve to clear away the toxicity. Continuing a pretense of not knowing what to do and demanding that the disenfranchised provide the solutions, which will be received with hostility and summarily ignored, only contributes to complicity with oppressive structures.

If you purchased this book hoping to learn how you can fix your complicity with racism, I'm afraid you just wasted your money. For you see, this book was not written *directly to* white folk. They are not the audience for this volume. This text was written to those who are among the least of these yet who remain precious in the eyes of God. White critics will no doubt dismiss me as some angry Latino or a race-hustler. Frankly, I have no interest or desire to waste my time in rebutting their characterization of me. I simply do not care, because it is my Latinx community and other marginalized communities to whom I am accountable and to whom I must answer. This book is for the ethnically and racially disenfranchised. My hope is to humbly suggest how those disenfrachised and I might respond to those who believe they are exalted, when in reality they will be among those demanding entrance to God's eternal rest only to be rebuffed. Regardless of all they did in God's name, still God never knew them.

Devotees of the dominant nationalist Christianity are not known by the God of creation, for they instead have clung to the illusion of the God of white supremacy. Therefore, if you read this book enfolded in whiteness, please note the following trigger warning: you will feel anxiety, defensiveness, anger, shame, discomfort, and stress. Some of you are likely to defend your actions, rushing to assert "we are really good people in spite of it all." But if you can work past your defense mechanisms, you will have the rare opportunity of hearing how communities of color speak among themselves whenever whites are not in earshot. You will have the rare privilege of eavesdropping on our conversation and looking over our shoulders to overhear perspectives you might never have imagined. What you do with all of this is totally up to you. Whether you choose liberation from racist sins is totally your choice. But as I said, your salvation is not the primary concern nor the purpose of this book.

By now, some of you are probably asking whether I, as

author, have a responsibility to raise the consciousness of oppressors and thus have an obligation to try to save white people from their folly. No doubt silence denies justice. But all too often, people of color are expected to "speak truth to power." This expression has always distressed me because it assumes power is ignorant of the truth and that there is the potential for redemption when truth is heard. And because the abused and misused know the truth, they must shoulder the burden of speaking truth to their persecutors, regardless of the consequences. I maintain that those in power know the truth all too well, yet still choose unjust and oppressive policies because they are profitable. I am not motivated to speak truth to power. I would rather focus on speaking truth to the powerless who have been taught for generations to believe the lie of those who shape our unjust social structures. Speaking truth with (not to) the disenfranchised raises consciousness and decolonizes minds, which can lead to praxis that might bring about change and maybe even change for the better.

Decolonizing Christianity is not an attempt to teach white people how to relate to those on their margins so that they can feel peace and serenity. Instead, these pages seek to demonstrate how dispossessed communities have believed the lie of white supremacy, which has relegated them to be among the least of these for our time. To an extent, this is an evangelical book reaching out to and seeking the salvation of people of color who carry the weight of indignity, whose very humanity has been denied by whiteness. This book is a call to those who are weary of racism and heavily burdened by ethnic discrimination. And if by chance those who are melanin-challenged, those who have also lost their own humanity by depriving humanness to those on their margins, were to discover their own salvation, then fine. We will celebrate this unintended consequence.

The Least among Us

The glaring incongruencies between whiteness and Christianity creates a cognitive dissonance that manifests in culturally destructive "shitstems" detrimental to communities of color. No other event of the new millennium best demonstrates the truth of James Cone's 1970 assertion that all white Christianity is satanic[1] than the 2016 election of Donald Trump to the presidency of the United States. The fact that most whites who identify as Christians voted for the antonym of everything taught by the Prince of Peace demonstrates that the one whom they worship is demonic. When a touch of madness led these white Christians to say that an avowed misogynist ("grab them by their pussies"), a committed racist ("there are good people on both sides" of Charlottesville's Unite the Right rally), a unapologetic xenophobe (Mexican migrants are "a people with lots of problems, bringing drugs, bringing crime, and being rapists"), and a habitual liar ("I'm a stable genius") is touched by God, then those who exist on the underside of white Christianity must have absolutely nothing to do with this white God, white Christ, white church, white ritual, or white spirituality. For the very survival, sanity, and salvation of people of color, this book will argue that this white Christianity must be rejected. The president they are worshiping, who is incapable of shame, must also be totally and completely rejected. Furthermore, if any hope exists for white folk's salvation, it can occur only through the God of the oppressed.

The underlying premise of this book is based on a passage of Christian Scripture found in the Gospel according to Matthew (25:31–46), better known as the parable of the sheep and goats. Before proceeding, we should pause and prayerfully read the following paraphrase of this passage:

[31] When the Child of Humanity returns in all glory, with the host of Heaven, they will sit on a magnificent throne. [32] All the nations will be gathered and be separated one from another as a shepherd separates the sheep from the goats. [33] The sheep will go to the right of the throne while the goats to the left.

[34] Then the one sitting upon the throne will say to those on his right, "Come, you who are blessed; take the inheritance that has been denied you, and enter now

9

into the eternal rest which has been prepared for you since the foundation of the world. [35] For I was hungry and you gave me food to eat, I was thirsty and you gave me water to drink, I was undocumented and you invited me in, [36] I was naked and you clothed me, I was infirm and you looked after me, I was in prison and you visited me."

[37] Then the just will reply, "When did we see you hungry and feed you, or thirsty and give you something to drink? [38] When did we see you undocumented and invite you in, or needing clothes and clothe you? [39] When did we see you sick or in prison and go visit you?"

[40] The one sitting on the throne will reply, "Truly I tell you, whatsoever you did for one of the least of these siblings of mine, you did for me."

[41] Then he will say to those on his left, "Depart from me, you who are cursed, into the eternal fire prepared for the devil and his angels. [42] For I was hungry and you proposed cuts to the Supplemental Nutrition Assistance Program, arguing it would make me too dependent upon the state and take away my incentive to work; I was thirsty and you refused to provide clean water in the Black neighborhood of Flint; [43] I was an undocumented immigrant and you built walls and threw my children into cages; I needed clothes and you tossed me in for-profit prisons for loitering and indecent expo-

sure; I was sick and you sought to repeal Obamacare and in prison and you fortified and widened the pipeline from Black and Brown schoolyards to prison yards."

44 They also will answer, "When did we see you as a welfare recipient, or living in Flint, or someone crossing our borders, or needing clothes or affordable healthcare, or in a prison disproportionately comprised of bodies of color and did not help you?"

45 They will hear as a response, "Truly I tell you, whatsoever you did not do for one of the least of these, you did not do for me."

46 Then they will go away to eternal punishment, but the just to eternal bliss.

Do not misconstrue this simple message. The difference between those who enter into their eternal rest and those condemned to exist separated from God was not determined by which faith tradition—or lack thereof—they proclaimed, nor which doctrines they believed, nor which church they belonged to, nor which aisle they walked down, nor which sinner's prayer they intoned. The difference between the saved and the damned is what they did or failed to do for the least of these. The political pronouncements of white Christians that ignore the cries of the nation's least of these are an outward sign of an inward rejection of the gospel. They are the ones, confused and indignant, asking, "When did we see you hungry and not feed you, or thirsty and not give you something to drink? When did we see you undocumented and cast you out, or needing clothes and did nothing? When did we see you sick or in prison and ignore you?"

So what are Euro-Americans to do? What is the solution they demanded I should have provided in my earlier book, *Burying White Privilege*? It's not complicated. Provide food for those who are hungry, give clean water to those who are thirsty, clothe the naked, welcome with open arms those who are undocumented, bring justice to the incarcerated, and provide medicine to the infirm. White Christian goats reject Jesus by the political policies they embrace and by voting for politicians who refuse to support or even acknowledge the least of these. Unravelling the social safety net, building walls to keep out those who are not white, and privatizing prisons and health care all become the outward expressions of hearts and souls that have rejected Jesus. Because most white Christians stand in solidarity with goats, for me to write a book seeking a new way to explain and present what has been obvious for over two millennia feels like a hopeless venture.

This book, as I already mentioned, is not written for Euro-Americans in the futile hope of shaming or encouraging them to do the right thing. For almost 250 years, white Christian terrorism has been the legitimized law of the land.

And while some white people were and might today be convinced to stand in solidarity with those who are abused by the supremacism of whiteness, unfortunately, a critical mass will not be achieved to bring about substantial structural and social changes that serve to create a more perfect and just union.

If the truth be told, the wealthiest among us are utterly poor, hungering to commune with those interested only in making more money, thirsting for acceptance for who they are and not what they possess, naked of life's simplicities. They are aliens to a world where 95 percent of the population exists in struggle because of the actions of the wealthiest. They are imprisoned behind gated communities and self-built walls, fearful of the other. And worst of all, they are infected with a virus that has sapped the ability to express empathy for the wretched of the earth. What then should be the spiritual, theological, and philosophical response? Those white people reading this book have received the incredible privilege and opportunity of reading words not intended for them, the privilege of listening in to a dialogue dealing with how those historically denied their humanity go about claiming their personhood. This book is thus a conversation geared toward and with US communities of color on how to deal with those who are on the left side of the throne.

Remembering Assumptions

Certain assumptions I made in *Burying White Privilege* are worth repeating here, because they will not necessarily be investigated in any great depth later in this book. First, white as an adjective to describe a satanic manifestation of Christianity does *not* signify skin pigmentation nor physiognomy. White Christianity refers to a worldview that embraces the supremacy of whiteness and believes in the manifest destiny of white bodies to occupy the highest echelons of power, profits, and privilege due solely to a light skin hue. True, many Euro-American Christians embrace this white and nationalist Christianity, but so do Christians who occupy bodies of color. A white Christian worldview can be advocated by those who are Black or Brown, Jew or Muslim, queer or heteronormative, atheist or humanist—anyone who defends the current unjust and unholy political, economic, and social power structures. The minds of those who do not possess white bodies and all they offer can still embrace white philosophical and theological paradigms, a means by which their minds become colonized. Therefore, the plea to "stop being white" is not a call to go to the tanning salon; it is a call to stop embracing a white worldview.

Second, no group of people is more responsible for the demise of Christianity than Eurocentric Christians, as demonstrated by the 2016 election in which 58 percent of

Protestants cast their votes for Trump, as did 60 percent of white Catholics, 61 percent of Mormons, and 81 percent of white evangelicals.[2] Most of those who insist they are followers of the dark-skinned Middle Eastern Jewish rabbi called Yeshua voted for a person who promised to make America great again by throwing this dark-skinned Yeshua-foreigner into a migrant camp. Regardless of the president's intentions, a good portion of his base recognize Make America Great Again as coded language for Make America White Again. Frightening for those on the margins is the fact that those who confess regular church attendance are more likely to be among Trump's political base of support than those who do not attend church. But white Christianity is dying. For the first time in US history, white Christianity is no longer the major religious expression of the white population. Only 43 percent of adult Americans identify as white Christians, and only 30 percent as white Protestants—numbers that continue to decline rapidly.[3] Maybe it's time to let the dead bury the dead.

And third, racism and ethnic discrimination are not simply blatant acts. They are more than engaging in the use of a racial or ethnic slur. They are more than wearing white sheets or burning crosses. Racism is an institutionalized ideology that creates and justifies unearned power, privilege, and profit for one group of people due to their race or ethnicity at the expense of others while systematically protecting, maintaining, and advancing said power, privilege, and profit. This institutionalized ideology is politically and economically manifested as white affirmative action, which ensures that discrimination protects access to education and jobs for less qualified white people. To describe racism and ethnic discrimination as ignorant feelings of superiority due to skin pigmentation creates a definition that helps the vast majority of whites benefiting from racist social structures to honestly believe they are not racist, and therefore they can express outrage and indignation if ever accused or questioned. Racists can really be nice, loving people who advocate colorblindness. Because they have a Black friend or an Indian grandchild, they are experts in the struggle as they speak over a person of color, hoping to educate that person on what racism might actually constitute. Racism is not a belief but complicity with an ideology. Annihilating this ideology is not learning how to be nice or more kind to people of color. Learning political correctness falls short. Bringing an end to racism requires dismantling the social structures that enforce the racism of nice, politically correct white people. More than simply tearing down statues celebrating Confederate soldiers who defended slavery, it also requires tearing down statutes like the electoral college designed to ensure political power to defenders of slavery's consequences.

One final note. Why does this book focus so much on

President Trump's metastasizing of America? After all, by the time you get around to reading this book, Trump might very well be a footnote in the dustbin of history as a new, more moderate president erases all of Trump's alt-right policies. Or we may very well be coping with four more years, thanks to his voting base coming out in force or the electoral college math delivering a second term. Or you might find yourself wondering how we got to the point of a third Trump presidential term. The thesis of this book does not depend on Trump being in office, even though much ink continues to be spilled on his account. We focus on the Trump presidency because probably no other president has wrapped himself so fervently in both the flag and the cross, merging the two with himself and the Republican Party. Archival film footage shows his creepy reach-around of the American flag as he hugged it, kissed it, and mouthed the words "I love you" after giving a speech at the Conservative Political Action Conference (CPAC) convention.[4] Then there is his retweet on December 28, 2019, of a meme of a white, muscular Jesus carrying luggage with the caption "[Obama] kicked me out—[Trump] invited me back."

Before Trump took the stage in Orlando, Florida, on June 18, 2019, to formally launch his reelection bid, his spiritual advisor, Paula White, asked the crowds to hold hands in prayer. She prayed that "every demonic network who has aligned itself against the purpose, against the calling of President Trump, let it be broken, let it be torn down in the name of Jesus! I declare that President Trump will overcome every strategy from hell and every strategy from the enemy—every strategy—and he will fulfill his calling and his destiny."[5] Whether we like it or not, white Christianity, for the foreseeable future, cannot be understood or analyzed apart from Trump's reshaping of Euro-American faith. This book focuses on Trump's unholy and unnatural connection to white Christianity to show how this symbiotic relationship demonstrates why many within communities of color continue to see white Christianity as, in the poignant words of James Cone spoken over half a century ago, "satanic."

2

The Day of Judgment

For centuries, a white nation was built on stolen land, with stolen labor, using stolen resources. The people of this white nation believe themselves to be self-made, pulling themselves up by their bootstraps, ignorant of how the wealth of the nation exists because of all that has been taken from communities of color. To maintain this oppressive system legitimized by laws, upheld by courts, normalized by schools, and ordained by Christian churches, people of color had to be defined as inferior, created by God to domestically serve those on the higher stages of the evolutionary scale. But it was never enough to simply relegate nonwhites to the role of servants. Structures needed to be created and violence committed to maintain the superiority of whiteness. Consequently, white Christianity became numb to the unacceptable suffering visited upon those who, in its opinion, fall short of whiteness.

Historically, the unscrupulous have been self-identifying as Christian, and more recently as evangelical, to mask all manner of death-dealing policies. Proclaimers of family values transgress against their professed ideals to embrace their worst impulses instead. The unraveling of safety nets—children locked in cages, the fortification of what Michelle Alexander calls the new Jim Crow, or the choice families face between medicine costing thousands of dollars and financial stability—demonstrates that "family values" is a meaningless bit of rhetoric serving as cover for unchristian commitments that glorify whiteness. Pontificating about the virtues of family values may feel satisfying and supportive of the good Christian life, but in fact it contributes nothing toward creating a more just social order.

This, of course, is nothing new. Eurocentric Christianity, since the days of Constantine, has predominately served as an apologist for authoritarian regimes, be they emperors, kings, crusading popes, or military dictators. In the last century alone, Eurocentric Christian jargon sustained and supported brutal regimes guilty of unimaginable human rights violations. Think of how the Catholic Church, fearing the loss of power during Spain's Second Republic, threw its support behind the right-wing politics of the usurper Francisco Franco, who cloaked himself as a defender of religious liberties. The church stood by him as he ignited a civil war against the seculariziation of society, turning a blind eye to the Spanish killing fields. Or recall how, earlier, the Catholic Church in Portugal supported the right-wing regime of Estado Novo, whose coup d'état against the democratic First Republic ushered in a reign of terror, again justified because he advocated family values. We also cannot forget that the rise of Hitler was aided by conservative Protestant Christians calling for *Ein Volk, ein Reich, ein Führer*. This is not to say all conservative Christians are fascists, nor that the left is innocent of harboring those who exploit secularism to impose intolerance. Multiple leftist dictatorships around the world are as oppressive as right-wing dictatorships. Still, the point is that conservative Christians have maintained a tolerance for family values promoted by authoritarian rulers who have engaged in all sorts of heinous injustices in Christ's name. If indeed Christ is the head of the church, and man is the head of his wife, then why be surprised when Euro-American Christianity celebrates patriarchy? What many of us find damnable is that proclamations of "family values" become the basis for a populist movement that is defining its family values by separating Brown families at the border.

White Christianity is now and has historically been an apologist for white nationalism. This is a Christianity that has failed to detect evil even though the faithful are staring directly into its eyes. The current spiritual leaders of Trump's political party don the religious garb of the persecuted and martyred while at the same time drinking from golden goblets filled with the abominable filth of spiritual adulteries. Rather than issuing a clarion herald for justice, Euro-American churches—all too often—are cults perpetuating whiteness by embracing a white God, a white Jesus, a white liturgy, white biblical hermeneutics, and a white theology reinforcing centuries of white supremacy. This supremacism established a white affirmative action securing the power, profits, and privileges obtained through the sweat of others' brows and the strength of others' arms. With white feet firmly planted upon land acquired through genocide, living in houses constructed through the enslavement of Black bodies, located within an empire carved out of the cheap labor and natural resources stolen from the Global South, white people lift their eyes to the heavens in thanksgiving to their white God, who richly blessed them according to the loving mercies God holds for "his" chosen. But woe onto us who lack faithfulness to whiteness, for this is a jealous God. How curiously different is this white God from the one preached by Jesus, who understood faithfulness by how we treat the hungry and thirsty, the naked and alien, the incarcerated and infirm. This white God of empire may be appropriate for global conquerors who benefit from all that has been stolen and through the labor of all those defined as inferior, but such a deity can never be the God of the conquered.

Complicity with Wolves

We live in a world where the president claimed by white Christians to be anointed by God ran a sham university, engaged in tax fraud through his charitable foundation, refused to pay contractors (forcing some into bankruptcy), engaged in housing discrimination, had ties with organized crime, paid hush money to a porn star to keep quiet about trysts during his wife's pregnancy, made lascivious comments about his daughter, and has been accused by seventeen women—and counting—of sexual misconduct. The impeachable offense of urging Ukraine, a foreign government, to open a bogus investigation of a political opponent was but one of the numerous high crimes and misdemeanors in which the president engaged. Add to the list, per the Mueller report and the Republican-controlled Senate Intelligence Committee report, collusion with the country's nemesis Russia for assistance in winning an election; or demanding his political critics be investigated and imprisoned while his convicted allies be pardoned; or even denigrating his own intelligence service while standing next to Putin, a hostile foreign leader. The magnitude of this president's statement, "I could stand in the middle of Fifth Avenue and shoot somebody, and I wouldn't lose voters"[1] begins to be grasped.

According to a January 2020 Pew Research Center study, even if Trump's crimes were proven without a shadow of a doubt, his guilt would still not be sufficient in the minds of his base to remove him from office. Thirty-two percent of Republicans and GOP-leaning voters, almost one in three Republican voters, say Trump "definitely" or "probably" engaged in illegal activities since he launched his campaign for the White House (as opposed to 63 percent of the total population who say the same). The majority of his base, 59 percent, believe that even though he committed a crime, he should not be removed from office.[2] Among Republican voters, the two subgroups that stand out for unwavering support, saying "there is almost nothing Trump could do to lose approval," are (1) those who primarily get their news and information from Fox News and (2) white Christians. Of white evangelicals, nearly two-thirds (63 percent) say Trump has not damaged the dignity of the office he occupies.[3] In the final analysis, virtually all white evangelicals (99 percent) and Republicans who watch Fox News (99 percent) opposed Trump's impeachment and removal from office.[4]

Trump brags that "no President has ever done what I have done for Evangelicals, or religion itself,"[5] and indeed he is correct, since the damage done may very well be irreversible. Nothing has become more important to white Christians than the transactional relationship of crying, "Caesar is lord" and in return having a space carved out for them within the political sphere from which they can exercise power. Winning becomes everything. Virtues and common decency are sacrificed on the altar of expedience. Two-thirds of white evangelicals believe their side is winning politically with Trump, according to a survey published by the Pew Research Center in March 2020. More than eight in ten believe Trump "fights for what I believe in," and 61 percent said the phrase "morally upstanding" best describes the president. And even though 70 percent of white evangelicals would use the phrase "self-centered" to describe Trump, a supposed sin—for Christians are called to put the needs of others first—they nevertheless embrace him because, as already noted, they are winning.[6] Winning outweighs virtue when white Christians embrace a consequentialist ethics where the ends justify the means—as opposed to the prescriptive ethics they have previously confessed based on ideal truths or principles.

Unlike Jesus, who refused Satan's temptations in the desert—the temptations of profit (bread), privilege (celestial protection), and power (all the kingdoms of this world)—nationalist Christians made a Faustian pact with Republicans for access to the very things Jesus rejected. Unchristian acts can be supported, or the core of Jesus's teaching can be rejected, so long as the white Christians are winning. For example, during the sixty-eighth National Prayer Breakfast, Arthur Brooks, president of the American Enterprise Institute, gave a moving tribute to Jesus's entreaty to "love your enemies" in the midst of the current "crises of contempt and polarization." Trump, speaking after Brooks, began his incendiary remarks by saying, "Arthur, I don't know if I agree with you. But I don't know if Arthur's going to like what I'm going to say."[7] As some cheered and whistled, he proceeded to lambaste, defame, and threaten his enemies with retribution for supporting the impeachment procedures. Vengeance is mine, saith Trump. Not surprisingly, some of his most sycophantic allies, like the Reverend Robert Jeffress, embraced Trump's tantrum. Rather than offering a humbled response on the difficulties of keeping Jesus's command to love your enemies (something all of us can relate to), Trump went on to repudiate the central teaching of the Sermon on the Mount. So, when 89 percent of white Christians believe the Bible should influence the laws of this country,[8] they are not referring to the Bible read by the disenfranchised, where the command to "love your enemies" is not up for negotiation. White Christian exegesis is instead based on a white, cisgender male perspective that constructs a religion ready and able to defend their unearned profit, privilege, and power.

The domestication and domination of white Christianity by the Trump presidency did not come about *ex nihilo*. There is a history to how this country arrived at this juncture. Likewise, ignoring this history only ensures the eventual rise of some future Trumpish president. The triumph of white, conservative, so-called family-values Christianity did not come about coincidentally. We can trace the current Trump Christian Age back to the 1940s movement that developed as a response to the New Deal and Social Gospel. The white Christianity of the mid-twentieth century sought to move the needle from the Social Gospel (Christianizing a savage capitalism that was crushing humanity) to the prosperity gospel (blessed are the faithful because they will be given health and wealth). The Social Gospel was rejected for a Social Darwinist Christianity—a survival of the spiritual fittest. Following the defeat of John Scopes, who was prosecuted for teaching evolution, white Christians retreated from public engagement, embracing a self-identity of sojourners not of this world. These Christians withdrew from politics, believing political structures were irredeemable. The focus turned to saving souls for the kingdom to come, not building allegiance with the powers, and principalities, and the rulers of darkness of this world. But a retreat from the chambers of influence never sat well with some. In back room prayer meetings close to rooms of power, a resurgence of nationalist Christianity was being meticulously planned and organized.

This resurgence started in December 1940 when more than five thousand titans of industry (the heads of such companies as Standard Oil, General Motors, Sears, General Electric, and Mutual Life) gathered at the Waldorf-Astoria Hotel in New York City for the annual meeting of the National Association of Manufacturers (NAM). They gathered as the nation was emerging from the Great Depression, resentful of powerful labor unions and government regulation of their industries. Until this meeting, these leaders and the nation at large had been told that the greed of capitalists was the cause of the 1929 economic collapse. The NAM tried to counter this narrative throughout the 1930s with appeals to Americans' self-interest, but this strategy had little effect or success. President Franklin Roosevelt shrewdly used religious jargon to sell his New Deal, which was picked up by liberal ministers throughout the nation and preached from their pulpits. During the 1940 NAM conference, however, one of the speakers—Rev. James W. Fifield—preached against the sins of Roosevelt's New Deal and the salvation that could be found in US free enterprise and deregulation. The titans of industry were not the cause of the Great Depression, Fifield proclaimed, they were the saviors. During his talk, Fifield—nicknamed "The Apostle to Millionaires"—suggested clergy would be the key to regaining the upper hand in the capitalist struggle against Roosevelt's liberal policies and dictatorial tendencies. This watershed moment made Christianity and capitalism soulmates in white America's imagination under the phrase "under God," which they then set out to popularize. Moving forward, the United States would henceforth be known as a Christian nation.[9]

J. Howard Pew, president of Sun Oil, along with his

brother Joseph N., despised Roosevelt and their former business competitor John D. Rockefeller, whose brand of ecumenism, interdenominationalism, and an international-ist Protestantism that prioritized science and reform, was leading the nation, they believed, toward secularism. Com-mitted to Christian libertarianism, they became patrons of Fifield's work by the mid-1940s, outsourcing the task of persuading citizens to embrace capitalist ideology to the church. Later, they would back an obscure tent-revivalist preacher and fiercely pro-capitalist named Billy Graham. Called by Pew, not God, Graham railed against all liberal social programs—the New Deal, the Fair Deal, the New Frontier, and the Great Society—during his crusades. Social ills such as racism would not be remedied by government, Graham preached. Their solution could be manifested only with the second coming of Christ.

The Pews were committed to using their petroleum for-tune to remake the Republican Party by driving out moder-ates like presidential nominee Wendell Willkie and replac-ing his ilk with libertarian conservatives.[10] The movement they financed, through Fifield's organization Spiritual Mo-bilization, maintained that once religious leaders realized they had something to fear from the "pagan stateism" lib-eralism of the New Deal, they would eagerly join the cap-italists in the battle for the soul of the nation.[11] Fear, then and now, remains a powerful motivator. Christianity and

capitalism, in their minds, were both merit-based. If you are
good, heaven is your reward; if you are bad, then hell is your
punishment. If you are good, you turn a profit; if bad, then
bankruptcy is your punishment. Wealth becomes a blessing
from God. This ordained order was threatened by the New
Deal, an evil that made government a false idol that needed
to be banished.[12]

Fifield prepared fertile ground for visionaries like Billy
Graham, Abraham Vereide, and Doug Coe, who went on to
merge US anxieties over the Cold War and an atheist Soviet
Union with the already established crusade against New
Deal policies.[13] They sought to more aggressively take back
their country for Christ, creating a vast nationalist Christian conspiracy to make converts in high places. They ce-
mented a nationalist Christianity that merged the state with
the growing power of a group of wealthy, white male capitalists who were steadfastly opposed to the Social Gospel. Their
goal was the Christianization of government, business, education, media, family, entertainment, and religion through
the creation of a quasi-democratic theocracy.

Since 1953, with the establishment of the National Prayer
Breakfast (called, until 1970, the Presidential Prayer Breakfast), under the theme "Government under God," a cadre
of powerful, white capitalists viewed themselves as wolves
chosen by God to create national, and then international,
Christian power centers where the white Christianity of

the powerful defined faith. By 1954, during the Eisenhower administration, the words "under God" were added to the Pledge of Allegiance and the slogan "In God We Trust" was added to postage stamps, followed by paper currency in 1955. (This phrase had already been placed on coins, on-and-off, since the Civil War.) In 1956, these words became the first official national motto. Eisenhower tried to move the discourse away from just conservatives to include liberals through talks of a "civil religion." Still, a cult of nationalist Christianity jelled and gained strength, which merged political power with the need to protect the wealth and privilege given by God to the few. This was a strategic move away from focusing on those whom Jesus called the least of these in favor of the chosen few.

The 1950s until the start of the new millennium was the golden age of white Christianity within the United States. The tentacles of nationalist Christianity spread and flourished under the tutelage of Billy Graham, Abraham Vereide, and Doug Coe—avatars for white capitalist men. These early religious superstars were called to strengthen a quasi-religious ideology that ensured the profit, power, and privilege of the few. With the Nixon administration of the early 1970s, a move away from Eisenhower's civil religion was in full force. Nixon, with Billy Graham's support, used Christian nationalism to divide rather than unite people by branding antagonists of his war in Vietnam or his administration as foes to Christian values.[14] The cultural wars that would consume the 1980s, bringing about national discord still being felt today, found their footing when Nixon and Graham separated the faithful (those committed to their cause) from the ungodly, secular unfaithful. Basically, white conservative Christians began to flex their political muscles to ensure the phrase "under God" referred only to them.

As the 1970s ended, the prevailing feeling was one of America in decline. The foreign and economic debacle brought about by a humiliating military loss in Vietnam, long lines to buy gasoline, and a hostage crisis in Iran all raised concerns that the US was a diminishing empire. Ronald Reagan ran on his 1980 campaign for president using the slogan "Let's make America great again." Ironically, this astrology-practicing divorcé who mastered the racist dog whistle, supported by the Religious Right, won the presidential election at the expense of the self-proclaimed born-again Christian president Jimmy Carter. Carter's problem was being the wrong type of Christian: a liberal who in retirement helped to build houses for the poor by hand. Reagan's victory was made possible with the mobilization abilities of a new white conservative movement called the Moral Majority, a group that, as we know, was neither moral nor a majority. Paul Weyrich, a commentator and religious conservative activist, was among the masterminds who created the Moral Majority, choosing Jerry Falwell to be the public face of the movement. In May 1979, Weyrich, along with Ed McAteer, a salesperson for Colgate Palmolive, and Alan Dye, an attorney charged with explaining the legalities of political movements, flew on a private jet to Lynchburg, Virginia.[15] Their original goals for the organization were to continue and expand what has come to be known as Nixon's "Southern strategy"—the use of racist, anti-abortion, pro-school prayer, and anti-LGBT sentiments to lead white Southern voters away from the Democratic Party and toward the Republican Party.[16] How was this accomplished? According to Falwell, the tactic was to "get them saved, get them baptized, and get them registered."[17] By the 1980s, Falwell had become a politically powerful Christian cultural warrior. He continuously gave calls to arms. White Christians should reclaim America, to "take back our children . . . take back our schools . . . take back our government . . . take back our Judeo-Christian culture." He preached that believers should not be on the defensive, but that like the early New Testament church, they should always be "charging the gates of Hell."[18] Through the Moral Majority, he led this charge in the culture wars, attempting to position white Christian conservatives as the exclusive voice on issues concerning godliness and virtue, specifically issues concerning family, education, and sexuality.

The glue that held the Moral Majority and conservative politics together was, and continues to be, white supremacy. Lee Atwater, an advisor to Reagan who would go on to become George H. W. Bush's 1988 campaign manager, best articulated during an interview how Republicans could win elections in the future: "You start in 1954 by saying, 'Nigger, nigger, nigger.' By 1968 you can't say 'nigger'—that hurts you, backfires. So you say stuff like, uh, forced busing, states' rights, and all that stuff, and you're getting so abstract. Now, you're talking about cutting taxes, and all these things you're talking about are totally economic things and a byproduct of them is, blacks get hurt worse than whites. . . . 'We want to cut this,' is much more abstract than even the busing thing, uh, and a hell of a lot more abstract than 'Nigger, nigger.'"[19]

As powerful as the Moral Majority was becoming, it was not enough, however. After the 1980 presidential triumph of Reagan, wealthy, conservative white Christians set out to reclaim the greatness Reagan promised in his campaign slogan. Flush with victory, a few powerful white ultracon-servatives envisioned an organization that would bring to-gether conservative religious, business, political, and me-dia leadership. On May 18, 1981, the Council for National Policy (CNP) was founded when 160 of the nation's leading conservatives gathered in the backyard of Richard Viguerie. Viguerie previously was the CEO of a right-wing fundrais-ing company that had secured millions for George Wallace's failed race-based 1968 presidential bid. Viguerie listed Sen-ator Joseph McCarthy of the 1950s as one of his heroes and made it one of his life's goals to end busing for purposes of desegregation.[20] Paul Weyrich, responsible for bringing the Moral Majority and Heritage Foundation into being, was another cofounder of the CNP.[21] Weyrich's goals were clear: "We are talking about Christianizing America. We are talking about simply spreading the gospel in a political context."[22] The CNP's first president was Tim LaHaye, coauthor of the popular Left Behind apocalyptic novels.[23] The three major financial backers of the organization were the Coors family (who made their riches in the brewery industry and provided the necessary seed money to establish the Heritage Foundation), the Hunt family (who tried to corner the silver market), and the DeVos family (cofounders of the pyramid-scheme company Amway).[24] Richard DeVos served as one of the early presidents of the group, and later his daughter-in-law, Betsy DeVos, served as President Trump's secretary of education. Her brother Erik Prince, the former CEO of Blackwater USA, started a for-profit mercenary army and has been accused of spying on US liberal organizations.[25]

Members of the CNP who had religious affiliations included Jerry Falwell, who made a name for himself by opposing Martin Luther King Jr., the Civil Rights movement, and the desegregation of schools. Other religious leaders enjoying CNP membership included strategist Ralph Reed, James Dobson of Focus on the Family fame, Don Wildmon of the American Family Association, televangelist Pat Robertson, Dr. James Kennedy of the influential Coral Ridge Presbyterian Church in Florida, Dr. Paige Patterson and Judge Paul Pressler, both of whom were the architects of the fundamentalist take-over of the Southern Baptist Convention, and Bob Jones III, former head of the university his grandfather founded and named for himself, which also prohibited interracial dating. Although CNP members' identities are kept strictly confidential according to their policy, and guests can attend meetings only with the unanimous approval of the executive committee, the Institute for First Amendment Studies infiltrated CNP and obtained its 1998 membership list, posting it on the internet.[26]

The CNP eventually and very successfully merged the antigovernment, low-tax fringe wing of the Republican Party with the Religious Right. A symbiotic relationship developed in which the business community provided financial funding for Religious Right grassroots organizations who in turn supported capitalist ideals. According to David Kirkpatrick, the *New York Times* reporter who was able to attend the CNP's August 2004 meeting, the group consists of "a few hundred of the most powerful conservatives in the country [who meet] behind close[d] doors at undisclosed locations . . . to strategize about how to turn the country to the right."[27]

But this turn to the right has met challenges due to the changing national ethos. With the start of the new millennium, white births began a steady decline to represent less than 50 percent of all births; same-gender loving marriages became the law of the land; law enforcement started to be held accountable for centuries of unrestrained harm and killings of persons of color as public demonstrations led to cries of defunding police departments; and white affirmative action began to be dismantled. Faith leaders who were once respected and had influence within society were being ignored and at times ridiculed. And to segregationists' dismay, a Black man occupied the White House. CNP members, and whites in general, felt their country slipping away from them. They no longer recognized the America in which they had grown up. They came to believe outsiders and welfare cheats were stealing their jobs and benefiting from social services paid for by white taxpayers. They became fearful for their world as their power, profit, and privilege became threatened. They demanded to again take back America, revising Reagan's previous slogan.

As voices from marginalized communities grew louder in holding white America accountable for its rhetoric concerning liberty and justice for all, white Christians grew resentful. They turned toward a Trump presidency to define what it means to be a Christian in today's America. Trump became, in their minds, the great, white hope for reclaiming perceived lost territory. Not surprisingly, a morally corrupt and bankrupted white Christianity bent their knees to the

K Street Jesus of a white nationalist culture. Through the glories of the new Rome the will of God would come about. Separated from his liberative teachings, Jesus became a mascot for white Christianity, merchandised as a spiritually impotent but commercially potent symbol.

While the focus of this book is upon the intersection of white supremacy and a nationalist Christianity that looked to Trump as the modern savior of capitalism in the ongoing battle against the New Deal, it would be an oversimplification to simply dismiss all of Trump supporters as racist (defined as having feelings of superiority because of skin pigmentation) even though they are racist (in complicity with structures that are racist in order to benefit their continued prosperity). More than being motivated by race-based arguments, some, specifically the wealthier within society, are motivated by class-based arguments, which fall along racial lines. No doubt the economic elite have been motivated to lend support to a racist candidate because of promised tax cuts, deregulation, and protectionism. A financial decision—which nonetheless has race-based implications—is also made by the downwardly mobile middle class, whose fantasies for upward mobility are fed by talks of saving coal-based jobs, bringing manufacturing jobs back from China, or closing the border to foreign job competition. Nationalist Christianity praises God for ordaining Trump. They see God's hand moving in US history and rejoice in the fusion and confusion of their political victories as God's victories. But the God who anointed Trump is the God of capital and the hand that is moving US history is the hand of the 1 percent.

The white Christianity proselytized by capitalism since the 1940s is not only life-denying for people of color; it is also a way of life that is, as we will soon explore, damning to most whites. So why would whites embrace the economic system peddled by those who economically benefit at their expense? Possibly, their racism runs so deep and the idea that people of color might also benefit from governmental policies is so galling that whites would rather vote against their own best economic and social interests than see any governmental assistance given to those who are not white. When the New Deal sought to protect its citizens with the first national minimum wage, unemployment insurance, the right to form unions in collective bargaining, and social security pension for the elderly, the only way Roosevelt was able to gain congressional support was to capitulate to Southern Democrats' demand to exclude nonwhites from several New Deal provisions. Decades later, the unweaving of New Deal safety nets was motivated by whites' resentment of nonwhites receiving any type of governmental benefits as best communicated by Ronald Reagan, the Great Communicator, and his mythical "welfare queen."[28]

The blinding hatred caused by racism and ethnic dis-

crimination is a more powerful motivator than any desire
to form a more perfect union in which whites' own standard
of living can be improved. Compared with other nations,
the United States's dismal standing in the world has much
to do with the historical successes achieved by nationalist
Christian ministers doing the bidding of the beneficiaries
of capitalism. When the US is compared with other industrial nations, we consistently rank at or close to rock bottom
on all indicators that measure human flourishing. Maybe
once, decades ago, the US was the leader in healthcare and
education, but now the United States, according to a study
conducted for the World Bank, ranks twenty-seventh in the
world.[29] In education, the US placed twenty-eighth out of
seventy-one countries in math scores and twenty-fourth in
science.[30] As reported by the CIA, according to the Gini co-
efficient, which measures income inequality while ignoring
other well-being qualifiers, the US ranks fortieth among 150
countries.[31] We are the only country in the Western hemisphere without a national paid parental leave benefit.

The United States is the only industrial country without
universal healthcare, spending more than any other country on substandard care ($9,892 with the world's median
at $4,033 in 2016).[32] We may boast about having a techno-
logically advanced care system, but access is reserved for
the elite few. Compared to other developed and developing
countries, the US ranks at or near the bottom when mortal-

ity and life expectancy are measured.[33] As I finish writing this book in April 2020, we find ourselves in a new chapter of global history with the spread of COVID-19. The coronavirus pandemic revealed that United States has a third-world healthcare system. Most of its citizens must deal with not enough virus tests, protective masks, and ventilators. In addition, we are among the few industrial countries with no federal law requiring paid sick days, forcing the infected to show up to work. Fear of losing income needed for food and rent outweighs the self-imposed quarantine needed to flatten the curve of the pandemic. The lack of paid sick leave, along with inadequate or no health insurance, helps explain why the United States quickly became the world's epicenter of the COVID-19 pandemic.

The United States has achieved first-place standing in one area, death. Whether we mean death caused by lack of affordable healthcare or death by an abundance of weapons, we as a nation who claim to follow the Giver of Life remain faithful to the Prince of Death. This death is not restricted to bodies of color, since the corporate greed of the 1 percent is truly color-blind. During the 2017–18 fiscal year, the US spent $649 billion on its military, more than what China, Saudi Arabia, India, France, Russia, the United Kingdom, and Germany spent combined ($609 billion). We can provide butter but choose bullets. If indeed this is a nation "under God," then this white God suffers from toxic masculinity, which seduces white men and women; this God is a prig who makes a preferential option for the instruments of war and death rather than care for human flourishing. This white God of death will continue reigning because "his" devotees are quick to vote for a lower quality of life rather than sharing the goods and benefits of society with fellow citizens of color.

Grabbing Lady Liberty

Tanks noisily rattling down the streets of Santiago heading toward the presidential palace where President Salvador Allende was holed up on September 11, 1973, represent how democracies used to be overthrown—with the blessing of the United States. Today, democracies do not fall with the sound of gunfire in the streets but through quietly passed legislation and subtler policy changes, which an apathetic electorate misses since they prefer shining entertainment over and against news. Military juntas of old are not to be feared as much as politicians elected by the people, who hold on to their power by teaching constituents how to fear the potential loss of their illusionary power, profit, or privilege. Vladimir Putin, Viktor Orbán, and Recep Tayyip Erdoğan become case studies on how the foundations of democracies are shaken to their roots by elected officials, who establish themselves as czars, emperors, and sultans masquerading as democratic presidents. Yes, they continue to reign over countries that are democracies in name only. Government of the people, by the people, and for the people is weaponized against those who dare challenge the ruling establishment.

The rise of white Christianity during the second half of the twentieth century was purposely designed to be non-democratic. Paul Weyrich, known as the "founding father of the conservative movement," the architect of the Heritage Foundation, and a leader of the Moral Majority, made it perfectly clear he was against the democratic principle of one person, one vote. During his address at the seminal Religious Right gathering in Dallas during the fall of 1980 he said, "I don't want everybody to vote. . . . As a matter of fact, our leverage in elections quite candidly goes up as the voting populace goes down."[34] In other words, when non-whites vote, white Christians lose, so we do not want *those* people voting.

Our gradually changing national demographics and younger adults' tendencies toward liberal views create an existential threat to conservative whites who fear for their inability to win future elections. The white Christian once-majority has become, in the last few years, a minority of the population. Forty-three percent of adult Americans now identify as white Christians, and only 30 percent as white Protestants.[35] As the nation becomes younger and more multicultural, Republicans remain predominately the white man's political party, increasingly representing the shrinking white, Christian, male, and rural elements of the US electorate. Republicans of the 116th Congress consist of 200 elected officials, of whom 95 percent were white and 87 percent were male. Compare this to the 235 elected Democrats who were 58 percent white and 62 percent male. Changing national demographics make national elections more difficult to win for Republicans, demonstrated by the fact that, since 1988, Republicans have won the majority popular vote only once out of the last seven presidential elections (the winner being George W. Bush in 2004 for his second term).

White Christians are afraid of no longer being the nation's dominant political party. They fear becoming a minority in the America of the future, which, if present demographic trends continue, will indeed occur. Fears of being erased, as voiced by tiki-carrying storm troopers in the streets of Charlottesville, throw caution to the wind as unholy alliances are made and hardball politics are played to establish an apartheid-style democracy. Whites embrace minority rule because they feel under siege by those historically disenfranchised groups who are demanding to participate in the fruits of the Republic. Legalized voter suppression, voter purges, closing polling places within communities of color, changing voter ID laws, racial gerrymandering, and attempts to place citizenship questions on the census have been carefully crafted and highly effective attempts to forestall the inevitable. And while the disingenuous explanation for these undemocratic practices has been called protecting the integrity of the voting process, President Trump, in a refreshing moment of honesty and transparency, confessed that if voting was made easier, "you'd never have a Republican elected in this country again."[36] Trump, like Weyrich before him, recognizes that those who have been demanding participation, regardless of how fair and just their entreaties sound, cannot be validified in the zero-sum minds of whites. Hence, the disenfranchised and those Euro-Americans who stand with them in solidarity must be vilified as the enemy, socialists trying to destroy Christian-based capitalist freedom and liberty through fraudulent elections.

Rather than referring to those who politically disagree as the loyal opposition or political competitors, Trump, early in his regime, labeled his opponents as enemies of the state, depicting them as "traitors" and "scum." During an October 2019 interview, referring to the "Never Trumper Republicans," he warned, "Watch out for them, they are human scum!"[37] Kicking off his reelection campaign at a rally in Orlando, Florida, in June 2019, he whipped up the crowd with these words: "Our radical Democrat opponents are driven by hatred, prejudice, and rage. They want to destroy you and they want to destroy our country as we know it."[38] For democracy to work, respect for differing political views is essential. Dehumanizing opponents creates an atmosphere in which violence becomes acceptable and desirable in order to right perceived wrongs. The caudillo stance, which dismisses any tolerance of political dissent, helps us understand why Trump fawns over Putin, Orban, and Erdoğan, an attitude particularly troubling since he engages in fetish dictatorial jokes, such as stating during some of his rallies that two terms as president will not be enough.[39] If indeed there is always an element of truth in jest, the base is being mentally prepared to entertain the idea of overturning the twenty-second amendment to the US Constitution.

Democracy functions in this country because of popular faith in the electoral system and the custom of losing an election with grace and dignity, as befitting a statesperson. Following the loss of an election, the candidate voluntarily vacates their office for the winner and goes home to prepare for a future campaign. Our government is expected to peacefully and summarily change elected leaders without protest because we accept that losing an election is part of our democratic process. Trump, breaking with these norms, warned his supporters and detractors alike of riots if he did not win the Republican nomination in 2016,[40] warned of a rigged election,[41] called for "Second Amendment people" to stop Hillary Clinton's Supreme Court appointments if she were to win the presidency;[42] warned evangelicals that violence would occur if Republicans lost the 2018 midterm election (fortunately no violence materialized);[43] and warned in a September 29, 2019, tweet of a civil war if he were to be impeached.[44] If Trump is true to form, it is only a matter of time before he or his base voices threats of violence concerning the 2020 election.[45]

A chaotic and cocky defiance along with outspoken disdain for the rule of law during the Trump years has been rooted in the president's undisciplined narcissism. And it matters not whether whoever follows Trump is an honorable person with profound integrity, the vulgarian-in-chief has so expanded the elastic powers of the presidency, has so weakened institutional safeguards, specifically in the State and Justice Departments, that the office is ripe for a more clever and skillful future politician with despotic illusions of grandeur to fully dismantle the fragile remnants of our democratic system. Trump may be gone, but like-minded political actors remain at all levels. Rather than hold Trump liable for high crimes and misdemeanors, which pandering Republican senators did not deny occurred during the impeachment trial, they played interference, petrified of a Republican base made in Trump's image who resonated with the president's lack of a moral compass. Even if this nation comes to its senses and renounces the blatant racism of the Trump administration, making a preferential option for a more genteel political manifestation, Trumpism, nonetheless, has laid the groundwork for a potential future in which a more sophisticated manifestation of white nationalism can better mask its xenophobia. The Trump presidency's enduring legacy, regardless of whether he is still in office as you read these words, will be the normalization of a nationalist Christian undemocratic morality for the twenty-first century.

The cosmic battle playing out in US politics is not between Republicans and Democrats, not between liberals and conservatives, but between democracy and theocracy. White nationalists seek salvation through the agents of empire. More important than democratic principles by which to live is humanity's desire to belong—which means that in the United States, one can belong to the most powerful empire the world has ever known. But this type of belonging is defined through one's relationship to whiteness and structures that benefit whiteness. For those with light skin pigmentation, their belonging faces little opposition. Regardless of the discrimination faced by the Irish and Italians at the start of the twentieth century, their light skin pigmentation facilitated their eventual assimilation into whiteness within a generation or two, an access denied to people of color, regardless of how many generations they reside within the United States. For those with darker skin pigmentation, belonging becomes nearly impossible to achieve. None belong until their words and deeds demonstrate a sufficiently colonized mind, best verified by how passionately they defend the structures maintaining white supremacy.

Democracy in the United States will not be overthrown by an invading foreign army. Heavy artillery need not roll down Fifth Avenue. Democracy's demise will be due to white nationalist Christians wishing to openly and publicly impose a dominion theology upon lethargic electors. The expiration of democracy has nothing to do with opposing that particular political system but rather with fear of losing one's predominance in a society where whites have always reigned. Demographic losses do not necessarily mean loss of power and influence, as long as an apartheid political structure is strengthened and reinforced. While the number of white Christians declines throughout the nation, their numbers are rising within the conservative Republican Party. Two-thirds of all Republicans now identify as white Christians as opposed to one-fourth of all Democrats.[46] The multicultural and multifaith demographic changes that favor Democrats are offset by the consolidation within the Republican Party of white Christians fighting hard to maintain their white affirmative action. Loss of white affirmative action explains why 68 percent of those who support Trump agree with this statement: "Today, discrimination against whites has become as big a problem as discrimination against blacks and other minorities."[47] Through the Republican Party megaphone, whites seek to continue defining Christianity in accordance with their white identity.

Bottom line: white supremacy and the Christianity it undergirds are incongruent with democracy. Voters dreaming upward seek solidarity with the 1 percent who share their skin pigmentation, even as that small minority pursues short-term gains by dismantling long-term democracy. The embrace by the top 1 percent of a narcissist who starves a nation so he can bask in his own image demonstrates how that 1 percent is less concerned with sustaining and strengthening the Republic than with lining their pockets. These neorobber barons continue appealing to white Christians to help them stay in power and increase their wealth through massive tax cuts and the deregulation of their businesses. This nationalist Christianity shaped to meet the financial needs of the privileged few is antithesis to democratic principles because of its selective patriarchal and hierarchal tendencies. As long as the head of the cult, the new Caesar to be worshiped, remains faithful to the political goals of nationalist Christianity, unquestionable devotion is demanded regardless of his moral failings. It does not matter if power is abused for personal gain. What matters is advancing the privilege of white Christians and dictatorially denying liberties to those outside the cult. The Bible says that "one cannot serve two masters, for they will love one and hate the other" (Matt. 6:22). For most conservatives, adherence to the cult of white Christianity has become a choice to love that which is antichrist (protection of power and privilege) and turn away from the God of mercy, the God who cares for the least of these. Those within communities of color are therefore tasked with wresting away from whites the supposed historical mandate to uncritically define what Christianity means in this nation.

The US Mortal Sin

US nationalist Christianity worships an unholy trinity, a tribal god created in its own white image. This trinitarian deity is part Moloch demanding the living sacrifice of their children to protect a contrived right to bear arms, part Tarhun leading his people in the quest to conquer others, and part Qetesh teaching people how to lust after what others have—their lands, their bodies, their minds. Worshiping false and violent idols requires embracing falsehoods. The US has chosen to celebrate ignorance over intellectualism, cruelty over compassion, and profits over prophets. Nazi Germany gave us *Lügenpresse*; Trump's America gave us *fake news*. Facts can be avoided or dismissed if we say they do not exist. A dystopian future is forged in which truths are exchanged for lies designed to privilege those who imagine themselves as repressed by political correctness. To lead economically challenged whites to support policies detrimental to their well-being, a person like Trump demands a suspension of reality. Reality becomes a construct agreed upon by those who have the most to benefit from that construct. Adherence to this constructed reality is maintained through misinformation and misrepresentation.

Reason and logic fall short in the face of conspiracy theories such as "immigrants are stealing our jobs." Such a statement is all that is needed to marshal passions and produce votes among the white masses. These conspiracy theories are subsequently repurposed as conservative truth and used to gaslight the general population and people of color. To resist conspiracy theories or refuse to suspend reality is to stand outside the white Christian cult, thus inviting ridicule. No matter how much of a family man 44 (former President Barack Obama) was, he is the one labeled an immoral dictator, even as 45 (President Trump) dismantles decades of democratic decorum. The capitulation of reason leads the misguided and mistaken to worship a thuggish ruler as God's anointed, one who ignores congressional subpoenas, dangles pardons before lawbreakers, and punishes those he perceives as lacking obsequious loyalty. Such pettiness was illustrated during the rising number who died from the coronavirus. In the midst of governors trying to get the federal government to provide assistance, the president instructed his vice president to ignore blue-state leaders (such as Governors Whitmer of Michigan and Inslee of Washington), who failed to show sufficient gratitude.[48]

Since the advent of the Trump administration, an age of vulgarity has settled upon the nation, now permeating all US culture. We have moved from the dog whistles of Nixon (the Southern strategy), Reagan (welfare queens and bucks buying T-bones with food stamps), and Bush Sr. (Willy Horton) to the outward embrace and defense of white supremacy by Trump ("there are good people on both sides"). Trump has exacerbated the nation's dysfunctionality and disunity caused by centuries of institutionalized racism. The very public partisan brawls between the right and left are but symptoms of a more critical ailment, a sickness that we as a nation continue to ignore or deny.

Within families, an open secret tearing the household apart that is never discussed usually results in dysfunctionality. Everyone knows about the infidelity or the substance abuse, but no one speaks of it, no one addresses the *white* elephant in the room. The *white* elephant in the room is how this nation was established on racist ideology of unexamined biases and unchecked complicity with institutionalized discrimination that influenced so much of our current political policies. Think of the electoral college that chooses our president, a racist system that undermines the one vote–one person rule by electing delegates whose names do not even appear on the ballot. The myth told to justify this undemocratic system is that representatives participating in the 1787 Constitutional Convention sought to protect smaller states from larger, more populous states that held too much power. In reality, the electoral college was formed as a compromise to give slaveholder states with small white populations a larger say in choosing a president by counting Black males as three-fifths of a man for electoral vote allocation, while denying Blacks the vote. Should we be shocked that five of the first seven presidents—all but those named Adams—were slave-owning Southerners? Racism is responsible for a system that has literally voided direct democracy in this millennium, leading to the ascension of two electoral losers during the first five elections—George W. Bush and Trump—who both lost the popular vote by five hundred thousand and 2.8 million votes respectively.

The division in this country is rooted in the refusal of the dominant culture to repent from its mortal sin—the establishment of white supremacy. This nation was founded with no desire to include nonwhites. Indians were annihilated so a nation could be built on their land. African labor was employed to build the nation whites had envisioned for themselves. The rise of an empire required the theft of resources and cheap labor from Latin America. Goods and labor could cross borders, but the bodies to which they were attached could not. Ignoring what undergirds the dysfunctionality of the family, or of the nation, in this case, will not postpone its inevitable exposure and rupture, as alienation and friction continue to fester. Perhaps a truthful conversation would lead to repentance, reconciliation, and recovery, but as a nation we have chosen to ignore the *white* elephant within our history and present day, which continues to lead to destructive behaviors and violent acts.

The dominant culture fails to see the link between the unearned privilege, profit, and power they accumulated and their current standing within society. Communities oppressed for generations are gaslighted into thinking they are the problem whenever they demand justice. The dominant culture wants people of color to finally get over their plight, without demonstrating resentment and anger. Like the abused spouse, they are expected to forgive, forget, and behave. Changing how social power operates or seeking a more just distribution of goods and resources is not now nor will it ever be up for serious discussion. The dominant culture refuses to confront its mortal sin, to examine or even acknowledge how whiteness—no matter how disenfranchised actual whites might be—still provides privileges over and against those who are not white.

Can We Talk?

Among the unexamined powers whites hold is the ability to establish the rules on how a conversation will unfold. They can direct the discourse so that the claims of those marginalized and disenfranchised can be dismissed as oversensitive, overblown, or overexaggerated. This setup offers little hope for honest conversation or even the notion of dismantling oppressive structures. The dominant white culture has the power to determine the discourse, decide which topics are addressed, set the appropriate tone for any conversation (to ensure the angry are silenced), and to decide which questions are proper to ask, what constitutes a correct response, and how to achieve and evaluate resolution. Those whose people have suffered centuries of grievances must abide by how the white culture constructs the discourse if they ever hope to have dialogue. If they are unable to comply, then the conversation must wait until they learn the proper ways to express themselves. But even if people of color jump through all the necessary hoops to be called civilized enough to engage in a respectful conversation with the dominant culture, the very words they try to use to convey their thoughts have been co-opted and used against them.

In an implementation of Orwellian doublespeak, the dominant white culture deliberately reverses the meanings of words meant to signify progressive concepts. A virtuous cause, for example "maintaining religious liberties," becomes "subjugating nonbelievers to the religious idiosyncrasies of the dominant group." Semiotician Ferdinand Saussure argued that words operate as linguistic signs, which do not unite a thing with a name but rather with a concept and an arbitrary sound-image. Saying "religious liberties" creates a complex sound-image, which as a mental notion masks and connotes relationships.[49] The understood meaning of "religious liberties," as an arbitrarily chosen signifier, creates a power relationship between those who redefined the term—white Christians (specifically males)—and those who are forced to accept the naming—marginalized communities. The linguistic sign "religious freedom" is a code that lets white men dominate the bodies of others by representing the supposed danger and threat that white male Christians face. This link between words and their interpretations becomes a well-established, unquestionable fact; and if fact, then society must take action to keep said threat at bay lest the safety and security of white male Christians be endangered.

Philosopher Michel Foucault argues that language is an "opaque, mysterious thing," which reveals as it conceals.[50] Language is more than simply a collection of words, because it constructs concepts while concealing repressive social structures. When the Justice Department under Attorney General William Barr prioritized religious freedom cases and provided special training to the department's lawyers, those attending the workshop soon realized they were being trained to blunt civil rights protection for gay and transgender people. Justifying the workshops, which is the first time such a workshop on any topic was ever offered, Barr said, "In my view, liberal democracy has reached its fullest expression in the Anglo-American political system. The well-spring of this system is found in Augustinian Christianity."[51] Also consider the Alliance Defending Freedom, a Christian legal group that in 2018 received $55 million in donations to fulfill their mission: the protection of religious freedom laws. Since its founding over twenty-five years ago, they have brought more than ten cases to the US Supreme Court to ban contraceptives and curtail LGBTQI civil rights. Among their most famous cases are *Masterpiece Cakeshop v. Colorado Civil Rights Commission*, concerning a baker's refusal to make a wedding cake for a queer couple, and *Burwell v. Hobby Lobby*, dealing with a corporation's refusal to provide birth control measures as part of a private insurance plan.[52]

Nationalist Christianity's use of the expression "religious freedom" reinforces white cisgender male supremacy within social structures designed to normalize oppressive policies imposed upon queers and nonwhites while legitimizing the supposed dangers they represent to white America. Linking the acoustic sign of "religious liberty" to such dangers aims to protect the antisocial qualities of nationalist Christians forced to go against their God when they feel forced to bake wedding cakes for gays or provide insurance coverage for contraception. Simultaneously, normalizing and legitimizing such "threats" against religious liberty give whites another reason to feel superior. The power to name makes it easier to control the object named. The power to name is crucial in justifying a white Christian nationalist social structure that perpetuates and protects white supremacy.

Eurocentrism has always had a knack for redefining words to signify the opposite of their original intent. These conceptual gymnastics, which would make any Cirque du Soleil performer envious, have defined the defense for Jim and Jane Crow as "states rights" or white affirmative action as "merit-based selection." How else can a people expounding the rhetoric of freedom justify acts that bring death, enslavement, and misery to so many? But these redefinitions have less to do with God and more to do with the imposition of patriarchal and heterosexual normativity upon a nation seeking liberation from the straitjacket of Eurocentric puritanical beliefs. Controlling the body of the female other or the queer other safeguards heterosexual male rights under the banner of "religious freedom." Unfortunately, while these Eurocentrists are advocating for domination of the other by redefining oppression as an assault on religious freedom, the federal government is staging a very real attack on religious liberties.

By insisting on religious liberties, nationalist Christianity curtails the religious freedom of those who have not been converted to their particular faith. Although the many white, conservative ministers leading the charge to take America back for Jesus do not say so, they are nonetheless embracing a uniquely US theological perspective, dating to the late 1960s, known as dominion theology. This theology gets its name from Genesis 1:28, where God, speaking to Adam and Eve before their expulsion from Eden, tells them that they would "have dominion over the fish of the sea, and over the fowl of the air, and over every living thing that moveth upon the earth" (KJV). Dominionism is a Christian political theology that advocates for the United States to be governed according to its proponents' particular understanding of biblical law. Specifically, they call for domination over the "seven mountains" of culture: government, business, education, media, family, entertainment, and religion. These seven mountains are based on Isaiah 2:2, which discusses "the latter days" when "the Lord's house shall be established on the top of the mountains."[53] These words, dominionists say, establish a biblical mandate for white Christians to control all earthly secular institutions—the seven mountains—until Jesus's second coming.

During the 1980s, the political theology of dominionism began to undergird the political advances of the Christian Right. According to sociologist Sara Diamond, dominion theology is "the *central unifying ideology* for the Christian Right," with adherents like Jerry Falwell.[54] Today's Christian cultural warriors building a hedge around Trump demonstrate the oversized influence of dominionism, which became more prevalent by the start of the new millennium, providing a theology justifying the occupation of secular spaces. Dominion theology is not a return to archaic Mosaic laws, which would, for example, reinstitute animal sacrifices; instead, it is an emphasis on how Christians interpret biblical principles for today's modern society. And while distinctions can be made between "hard" and "soft" dominionists ("soft" does not advocate replacing the US Constitution with biblical law, while "hard" does), both agree on the supremacy of white Christianity and its rightful place to rule. Whether flaccid or erect, dominionism is an existential threat because it seeks to ban LGBTQI civil rights, reproduction rights, women's equality protections, secular education, contraception, and most important, religious freedoms safeguarding a plurality of faiths. Their vehement objection to the nonthreat of Muslim Shariah law within the country was not based on a conviction concerning church-state separation. Rather, they believe this separating wall should be demolished so that the state could be guided by the church, for they believe the nation's founders never intended such a wall. They do support implementing a type of Shariah law, as long as the emphasis is on Christian nationalism and not Islam. During the 2016 presidential election, Senator Ted Cruz, according to historian John Fea, was the dominionist candidate.[55] Rick Perry held that honor during the 2012 election. And while Trump may fail to convince most thinking adults that he is a Christian, there should be no doubt he has strong ties with and is dependent upon the votes of dominionists. For them, religious freedom becomes coded language to impose a dominionist type of liberty exemplified by Kim Davis, the Kentucky county clerk who refused in 2015 to issue marriage licenses to gay couples in accordance with a US federal court order because it violated her "religious liberties."

Other words besides *religious freedom* have been redefined to justify the opposite of what they signify, words like *justice, reconciliation, salvation,* and *liberation.* White Christians have co-opted these words, changing their meaning from what has been historically understood by the world's marginalized. These words come to describe a Eurocentric, unjust, divisive, damning, and oppressive drive. On the other hand, embracing an epistemological privilege for the oppressed means that only those who are disenfranchised get to define how these terms are employed. Those who have benefited throughout history by redefining these terms to justify everything from indigenous genocide to today's border policies can never be entrusted to either define these terms or supervise their implementation. As beneficiaries of a dominion theology that they have philosophically and spiritually legitimized, normalized, and legalized, Euro-Americans remain incapable of seeing the reality of those on the underside—because they wear the mask of whiteness, which provides the safety of inclusion in their religious cult.

Unfortunately, whenever issues of justice, reconciliation, salvation, or liberation are explored, they are elucidated from the perspective of present power structures. Such simpleminded studies usually lead white churches or white denominations to offer public repentance for their racism, asking for public forgiveness, making symbolic changes, and encouraging public reconciliation for past racist sins. These are empty gestures that seek mainly to soothe the guilt of white souls without changing or challenging the privileges that are embedded within white bodies. These gestures focus on how whiteness can feel good about itself without forsaking any of the advantages with which it is associated. This Euro-American Christianity reduces acts of justice, reconciliation, salvation, or liberation to an expression of pity for the unfortunate who need charity. Such paternal expressions of disingenuous contrition change nothing. Euro-American Christians prefer nothingness over and against disenfranchised people themselves seizing the power to define justice, reconciliation, salvation, and liberation; for if they do, then radical political, economic, and social changes become prerequisite to establishing a new social order.

Redefining words supports the dysfunction of a nation

where those who benefit from oppressive structures preserve the power to claim victimhood. Rather than recognizing that they are recovering racists, they feign righteous indignation when their racism is called out. Offended, white Christians are aghast when they are accused of being racist, since they see themselves in Lacan's mirror as embodying the very essence of "truth, justice, and the American way." Intoxicated with visions of supremacy, they become the light set upon the hill, a beacon shining the truth of Jesus Christ to a world lost in darkness. So, when those relegated to the underside question the integrity of white people's faith, whites are incredulous. Rather than considering the perspectives of the marginalized, they gaslight communities of color into believing they, white people, are the true victims. More than four in ten (42 percent) Americans believe discrimination against whites is more pervasive than discrimination against people of color, and more than one-third (36 percent) believe that "immigrants are invading our country and replacing our culture and ethnic background."[56] Almost half of the white population (49 percent) believes so-called "reverse discrimination" is real (even though no empirical evidence for it exists).[57] This type of white Christian gaslighting denies the disenfranchised the reality of their experience and takes away their control over their narrative, which in turn destabilizes their worldview.

White Christians, as the so-called "true" victims, are liberated from having to deal with how social structures were designed to privilege them. They maintain they are the only ones who truly "belong" to the United States, and everyone else, regardless of how many generations they have occupied the land, simply live here. People of color simply live under the illusion they belong. Whenever people of color try to begin a conversation on how the marginalized can also participate in the fruits this country offers them as full and equal citizens, those whose power, privilege, and profit are jeopardized cast themselves as the real victims, labeling dialogue-seekers as agitators, socialists, or race hustlers. White Christians define themselves as living under the tyranny of those who have been historically oppressed but who now, possessing unfair advancement opportunities, are blaming whites for all their shortcomings. Unleashed white rage toward those who dare to push back against oppression is one of the many privileged activities of being white. The ability to pound tables, feign self-righteous indignation—in short, to pull off a Brett Kavanaugh when confronted with their embrace of cisgender male supremacy—is all whites need to sweep abuses under the rug. Their fear of losing their place within society, of being erased, leads to the metanarrative that if people of color are given the chance, they would politically bully white Christians into submission.

No doubt, part of their fear might be based on the false assumption that the descendants of those who suffered under white Christian terrorism since the foundation of the Republic are planning to repay violence in kind once they become the majority. When hordes of Europeans invaded what would come to be known as the Western hemisphere, they stole, raped, and murdered everything in their path. For this reason, whites fear that when they become the minority, communities of color will oppress whites just as they were once oppressed by whites. They project onto people of color their own proclivity to participate in crimes against humanity. "Jews will not replace us" becomes the battle cry at the Charlottesville "Unite the Right" rally. Their fear of becoming the new oppressed may explained their brutal policies designed to thwart shifting demographic trends, even if it means the unconscionable act of confining children to cages. This trajectory toward minority status, they believe, which began with Obama, was stopped in its tracks with the appointment of Trump to the presidency by the electoral college. Yet ironically, because whites impose upon bodies of color their own character traits and tendencies, they are, in fact, fearing themselves—or as the great philosopher Pogo once quipped, "We have met the enemy, and he is us."

3

Accompanying the Least of These

Historically and currently, white Christian behavior indicates an incapacity for empathy and sympathy for communities of color. The collective narcissism of the exceptionalism voiced by this nation shares a kindred spirit with the narcissist-in-chief. American exceptionalism today is the twenty-first century reincarnation of the divine rights of kings. The most powerful empire the world has ever known, the new Rome of our age, reserves for itself God-like powers over those subjugated to its will—powers over life and death, powers to create truth, powers to punish the peccadilloes of those who threaten their rule, powers to demand devotion—in effect, powers to dismantle democratic principles. This superiority, not surprisingly, includes a racial component.

Eurocentric nationalist Christianity was never a spiritual way of being. Instead, it was a philosophical justification for unchristian governmental policies. Since making their Faustian bargain for the sake of political influence and expedience, the prevailing white Christianity of the United States became the advocate and ally of this, the new Rome, in exchange for a place at Constantine's banquet table. For centuries, the predominant religion of this nation maintained certain political structures to sustain white supremacy. This is and always has been a false Christianity, a political ideology that has captured the hearts and minds of those occupying the highest echelons of political power; it has been a cruel and callous religious ideology that has found its fullest manifestation to date in the presidency of Donald Trump. Maybe the reason white Christian America is so quick to forgive Trump's lack of scruples and shamelessness is that the majority of his devotees find in this sinner a refuge for their own unrestrained lust for power, profits, and privilege. Regardless of whether 46, whoever that may be, seeks to undo the harm inflicted upon the nation by 45, the fact that 45 existed in the first place confirms and continues the United States's slide toward Sodom.

The story of Sodom, according to the biblical text, has nothing to do with same-gender loving relationships. The prophet Amos (4:1, 11) condemned Sodom for "oppressing the poor and crushing the needy," and Ezekiel (16:49) claimed divine punishment was for the "city's unwillingness, due to pride and haughtiness, to share their abundance with those who were poor and marginalized." God did not rain fire and brimstone upon the city because of homosexuality, as many homophobic preachers continue to proclaim. God's divine wrath was unleashed because of how the inhabitants treated their least valued and most vulnerable members of society. The United States is thus no less guilty of Sodom's sin. White Christianity is the religion of modern-day Sodomites because of how the nation, under the cover of faith, cruely treats the hungry and thirsty, the naked and alien, the incarcerated and infirm. Either God's judgment must one day rain down upon white Christianity, or God will certainly owe Sodom an apology.

Building Hatred

Jesus's encounter with the Canaanite woman (Matt. 15:21–28) always perturbed me. Why? Because Jesus rejects someone asking for her daughter to be healed because of her ethnicity. Canaanites during the time of Jesus, like Latinxs today, were scorned for lacking purity and were perceived to be a mongrel race of inferior people. The Canaanites then, like Latinxs today, were considered a people with lots of problems, bringing drugs and crime to the region and also being rapists. Not only did Jesus reject this Canaanite woman; he also called her a bitch. Whenever I read this story, I find myself more in solidarity with the Canaanite woman than with the one whom I claim to follow. After all, it is today's Latinxs who are the dogs of society, the bitches of whites. I am old enough to remember restaurant signs throughout the southwestern United States that would read, "No dogs, no Mexicans." In Miami, real estate signs during the 1960s once read, "No Blacks, No Cubans, No Dogs." But we do not need to look back sixty years to see how Latinx people continue to be relegated to being society's dogs. We just need to consider that five Brown bodies perish every four days attempting to cross the desert on our southern border.[1]

Jesus's denying the Canaanite woman a chance for her daughter to be healed and then calling her a bitch relegated her to the underside of her society. How much worse has this nation done by institutionalizing oppression and violence toward Latinxs, the dogs of our society? Calling people dogs because of the ethnic group they belong to creates a xenophobic environment ripe for vigilante retribution. Since Trump began campaigning in 2015, we have seen a spike in hate crime, threats, and attacks perpetrated by Trump supporters who (1) explicitly declared support for Trump or used his slogan while engaged in a violent act or threat; (2) cited Trump or his rhetoric as justification for the violence or threat given; (3) committed or threatened violence toward opponents of Trump while at Trump events or wearing Trump paraphernalia; and (4) declared allegiance to Trump prior to committing or threatening violence toward Trump's opponents.[2] And while many hate crimes can be directly related to Trump's anti-Latinx rhetoric, many others have been inspired without necessarily invoking his name.

Upon this rock of hatred Trump has built his church. He has mainstreamed the rhetoric of formerly fringe hate groups who have found a voice and platform in his administration and on right-wing media outlets. The white nationalist hate groups' theme of fighting their perceived displacement by Brown and Black people is often echoed by Fox television personalities like Tucker Carlson and Laura Ingraham. With 1,020 hate groups surging in the United States since 2016,[3] xenophobic acts and thug violence are the new political norms. As a Latino man, I am more afraid now than I have ever been during the sixty plus years I have lived in this country. Since 2016, we have moved from a society held in check by political correctness, which poorly masked ethnic discrimination and racism, to acts of outright revenge against communities of color. And while individuals are not responsible for hate crimes conducted in their name, Trump has systemically used enough anti-immigrant rhetoric and anti-Latinx stereotypes to make his most ferocious fans foam at the mouth. While anti-Muslim violence due to the fear of terrorism peaked in 2016, the shift to fear of immigrants as the new danger has increased violence toward Brown people as they become the newest scapegoats.[4]

Violent hate acts are not limited to individuals. The bloodshed perpetrated by ruffians on the streets, as incited by our leader in the White House, leads to the democratization of violence. To safeguard whiteness, the government has legitimized death-dealing policies toward those outside of the protected class. Unlike the random assaults by single perpetrators that Latinx people might face on the streets, this institutionalized violence established by the government in the form of immigration policies is not random. It becomes an effective component of society when it functions within a legal framework designed to promote the alienation of people of color, their economic devastation, and their early deaths. This violence, drawn out over years, if not decades, is caused by millions of microaggressive papercuts and at times straight-out macroaggression.

Spewing paternalistic rhetoric while eating taco bowls on *Cinco de Mayo*, the Trump administration, for whom a majority of white Christians (evangelical, Catholic, and mainline) voted, has institutionalized and normalized hatred for Latinx people. *Hate* is the best word for the severe loathing demonstrated by the Trump administration and reflected by so many of his enthusiasts, who gleefully chant, "Build that wall!" Claiming divine calling and political exceptionalism, they preach a gospel of hatred—a hatred that disfigures humanity by denying the least of these any share of the fruits of creation.

Hatred has always been a powerful manipulative political tool used by petty despots to persuade those seeking unsophisticated answers to complex questions. Latinxs have become the wedge issue politicians use to focus the anger of the downwardly spiraling white middle class. "I too could have been financially independent if it wasn't for those damn sp*cs taking my hard-earned American jobs!" Yet this same struggling white middle class has more in common with communities of color who are also struggling to survive than with the wealthy 1 percent who share their same skin pigmentation. Anti-Latinx and anti-immigrant wedge politics continue to whip up a frenzy of fear and hate toward those who clean white people's houses, take care of their children, and attend to their elderly. We are the only nation that demonizes those who harvest our food. This fear was displayed during the early stages of the spread of the coronavirus throughout the United States. Since late January 2020, the one who had been previously scaring whites with tweets about "caravans" of Brown people making their way to the border stated that he was considering sealing the border with Mexico as a health precaution, even while during this time he ignored warnings about the virus costing lives, admitting, "So I said to my people, slow the testing down please."[5] By early March the United States had a little more than eight hundred cases of COVID-19 with thirty deaths.[6] "We need a wall more than ever" as a remedy to the virus,

Trump tweeted. But the entire nation of Mexico during the same period had only six confirmed cases.[7] So which nation is more likely to be infected by their neighboring country? Since then, it was Mexico that demanded a crackdown on infected US citizens crossing the border to buy up Mexico's supplies in preparation for the shelter-in-place directives. In an ironic twist, Mexicans wore face masks and held signs telling Americans to "stay at home."[8]

Still many, like the president, appear excited by the idea of building walls, fantasies that might come true if connections can be made between dirty and disease-ridden Brown bodies and the protection of Euro-Americans' health. Making such linkage was Ohio state senator and physican Stephen Huffman, who proposed that "the colored population do not wash their hands as well as other groups."[9] Hatred never lets the opportunity afforded by a crisis slip through its fingers if it can advance making life miserable for the object of hatred. I do not exaggerate this hatred, nor am I oversensitive. When Trump rhetorically asked a crowd during a May 2019 rally in Florida how the US Border Patrol might keep migrants from crossing, a heckler shouted out, "Shoot them." The president chuckled, a chuckle heard by twenty-one-year-old Patrick Crusius. Three months later, Crusius walked into an El Paso Walmart to hunt and shoot people who looked like immigrants. Twenty-two died and twenty-four were injured.

Whites may profess to love Jesus, but they certainly hate Jesús. Jesús, crucified outside the city walls, dies in radical solidarity with all migrants being crucified outside the border walls. The Christians who claim their faith is the reason they support Trump and his sadistic and satanic immigration policy are worshiping a similarly sadistic and satanic white Jesus. Trump-voting white Christians are denying humanitarian aid to the least of these. Is this civilized? Technological and scientific advances become void when a monstrous people ignore basic tenets of decency and humanity. But what can we expect of people with an unexamined history of reaching economic heights by standing on the necks of Indians, whose lands they stole through the quasi-religious justification of manifest destiny? What can we expect of people who stole African bodies, enslaved them, and gained riches from their labor under the quasi-religious justification of Christianizing a perceived primitive people? What can we expect of people who have stolen raw materials and cheap labor from Latin America through the quasi-religious justification of the White Man's Burden? And how ironic is it that people who have enriched themselves through massacres, slavery, and bloodshed—and who are the latest immigrants to this land—would rewrite themselves into the national narrative as the victims of our current immigration crisis?

We have an immigration crisis because the latest immigrants to this land—white Europeans—created the crises. Undocumented people attempt hazardous crossings because of harsh twentieth-century US foreign policies and trade deals. Economic conditions created throughout the Caribbean basin push immigrants out while the US hunger for cheap labor pulls them into the United States. A century of US military intervention provided freedom for US corporations (like the United Fruit Company) to build roads into developing Latin American countries to extract, by brute force if necessary, their natural resources and cheap labor. Why then should we be surprised when the inhabitants of these same countries, this author included, would travel these same roads to follow everything stolen from us? The reason I am an immigrant in this country (once designated by the racist term "illegal") is because I am following all that has been stolen from the land of my birth—my sugar, my tobacco, my rum—the three necessities of life. The US created the immigration crisis yet refuses to recognize its culpability. We come escaping the poverty, violence, and terror the US historically unleashed upon us through gunboat diplomacy and regime changes in its effort to protect *pax americana*, the needed status quo for American businesses to flourish.

Gaslight the immigrants into believing they are the illegals. This is a better strategy than dealing with the historical illegalities of creating banana republics. Governments south of the border—at times democratic governments—were routinely overthrown to install military dictators who would ensure that the business interests—bananas—of US corporations were protected. But while conservatives call and treat us like dogs, liberals are no better with their call for hospitality. They ignore that the virtue of hospitality assumes the house belongs to the ones practicing this particular virtue who, out of the generosity of their Christian hearts, are sharing their resources with the other, who has no claim to the house. But it was Latin America's natural resources and cheap labor that built this US house in the first place. Due to US-sponsored banana republics, Latinxs hold a lien on the title of this US house. A debt is owed. Rather than speaking about the virtue of hospitality, it would be more accurate to speak about the responsibility of restitution. Maybe the ethical question we should ask is not, "Why are they coming?" but, "How do we begin to make reparations for all the US has stolen while creating the present economic empire?"

So what about Jesus calling this woman of color a bitch? How could such xenophobic words proceed from those deified lips? In the fullness of his divinity, Jesus had to learn how to be fully human. His family and culture were responsible for teaching him how to walk, how to talk, and how to be potty-trained. He also learned about the superiority of his people and the inferiority of others in the very same way that Euro-Americans, from childhood, are taught the

US is superior to other countries, and this is an exceptional nation. Jesus was willing to learn from this woman of color. And thanks to her, his ministry was radically changed, becoming inclusive from that day forward. Her response shocked Jesus into realizing faith was not contingent on a person's ethnicity. In fact, Jesus had to admit this woman possessed great faith. It was unimportant whether she belonged or had proper documentation. She was willing to cross the borders erected to separate her from Jesus because of her gender and ethnicity. Why? Because her daughter was sick and was entitled to be healed. She was more than the dog Jesus called her—and so too are Latinxs today!

Building Walls and Cages

It is incongruous for a person who claims to have faith—faith in a deity, faith in humanity, faith in oneself—to silently support legitimized, callous acts of tearing infants from the arms of nursing mothers, whether for the purpose of selling them for profit to a plantation, placing them in Indian schools, or deterring immigration. Normalizing the casting of toddlers and children into concentration camps built just for them in places like Tornillo, Texas, can occur only if beating hearts of flesh are turned to stone. How else can one make sense of white Christians sitting idly by as Latinx children are ripped from their parents' arms and placed in cages to sleep on dirt floors or are bundled into a caged room with a hundred others? And while one could argue that not all Brown children end up in cages, such deflections obscure the fact that in 2019, some 69,550 Brown children—children, for God's sake!—were in government custody.[10] One child detained, no matter how gilded is the cage, is one child too many. Such actions are sufficient to indict an entire nation for its pride and haughtiness.

We detain more children than any other nation, making us number one in another death-inducing category. Take the example of a three-year-old Honduran girl, torn from her father in March 2019 and placed in foster care, only to be sexually abused before being deported back to Comayagua. According to the September 2019 issue of *Pediatrics*, the journal of the American Academy of Pediatrics, detained migrant children "face almost universal traumatic histories." Such child trauma causes toxic stress associated with higher rates of depression, post-traumatic stress syndrome, anxiety, cancer, heart disease, self-harm, and even early death.[11] But there is money to be made in destroying the lives of Brown children. For-profit prisons, according to the US Department of Health and Human Services, charge up to $775 per child per day to house one hundred youngsters in a single room (more than when families are kept intact).[12] This little Honduran girl is but one of the thousands of traumatized youngsters who will be haunted for their rest of their lives thanks to anti-Brown US policies of deterrence. The norm-bending Trump presidency of chaos and "covfefe" has stunted any possibility of Latinx human flourishing for many. We are less than dogs, for at least dogs are treated more humanely. Think of Sarah B. Fabian, a lawyer for the Justice Department, who during a federal case before the US Court of Appeals for the Ninth Circuit in San Francisco on June 2019 argued against providing soap, toothbrushes, or beds to detained migrant children because it was not part of the government's responsibility to ensure "safe and sanitary" conditions.[13]

Our current immigration policies follow the long, immoral pattern of a nation in which mass killings, mass theft, and mass incarceration befell those falling short of the white ideal. In the midst of death, Christian churches are called to be messengers of love and hope; but regrettably, their complicity with the rulers of this world has led to a colossal failure in the implementation of the teachings of Jesus. Fear and hatred created these death-dealing policies, and churches responded by not caring. Instead, white churches hide behind flowery religious platitudes. Their acts of omission and commission have much to do with their indifference toward the least of these. Their apathy is simply criminal. One cannot be among the sheep on the shepherd's right side and remain silent as the Latinx young are subjected to a trauma that will carve psychological scars upon their impressionable, innocent minds. Guards at for-profit prisons may be able to rinse away the stench of the unwashed incarcerated bodies of undocumented children that clings to their clothing, but they, and the nation they represent, will have greater difficulty cleansing their souls from the odious harm caused by caging children.

Silence, from humans or deities, is maniacal complicity. White privilege, despite protests to the contrary, embraces a deafening quietness that masks consent with the racist stereotypes upon which Trump launched his campaign and has executed his presidential responsibilities. White supremacy provides ethnonationalist Christians with the excuse they need to vote for Trump, in spite of xenophobic tweets. One cannot be a person of faith while supporting anti-Latinx immigration policies or the man calling for their implementation unless, of course, that faith is in the supremacy of whiteness and the God created in the image of whiteness. Goats professing a faux faith are relegated to the shepherd's left because they specifically chose to privilege their white fur rather than to hear the cries of the hungry, the thirsty, the naked, and yes—the alien in their midst.

It is naive to think Trump's policies are solely targeting those whom he calls "bad hombres"[14] to keep America safe. Latinx of good faith are being victimized to keep America white. Among those being relegated to our modernized concentration camps are the highly educated, taxpayers, and entrepreneurs. Many have served their adopted country's armed forces, shedding their blood on the battlefields of Afghanistan and Iraq. They have risked their lives rushing to save others in numerous national disasters, from collapsing towers in New York to hurricanes named Harvey, Katrina, Maria, and Donald. It is naive to think Trump's barbarous immigration policies are somehow protecting the rule of law. In this case, "law and order" signify immigration policies designed to privilege white bodies at the expense of Brown bodies. *Everyone* who occupies a Latinx body, regardless of documentation, is illegal until proven innocent. Our very being places us outside the law where our rights are denied and our lives endangered by trigger-happy Trump-supporting vigilantes, some of whom wear the uniforms of police and border agents.

The Trump administration seeks the erasure of Brownness even if their disappearance economically hurts the entire country. On March 2019, our sadist-in-chief ordered the shut-down of the two-thousand-mile border with Mexico by noon the next day, oblivious to such consequences as trapping American tourists south of the border, stranding schoolchildren, and triggering an economic meltdown on both sides. The president then publicly announced a variety of juvenile solutions such as digging a water-filled moat along the wall and filling it with snakes and alligators, causing his aides to scramble for cost estimates to make the president's fantasies a reality. The president also advocated that border agents shoot migrants who allegedly threw rocks at them, something already occurring with impunity even when rocks aren't thrown, such as the senseless murder of sixteen-year-old José Rodríguez.[15] White House leaders informed the president that such actions were illegal. But concerns about legality did not deter him as he sought a work-around, suggesting that migrants be merely shot in the legs. Aides who resisted these ideas were fired by week's end.[16] This hatred geared toward a particular group of bodies defined as Brown who lack proper documentation was expanded by our current head of state to encompass all people of color. Rather than deterring Brown bodies from crossing physical borders, the national ethos is aimed at all bodies of color, seeking to deter them from crossing invisible borders separating them from the privilege, profit, and power afforded by whiteness.

Such a prevailing culture of cruelty leads whites who consider themselves good Christians to participate in demonic acts in the name of Trump. Many who leave for work, kiss their spouses goodbye, pet their dogs, and drop their kids at daycare have engaged in monstrous deeds simply because they have been federal employees during the Trump administration. Think of the federal officer carrying out Trump's "extreme vetting" executive order by handcuffing a five-year-old boy and separating him from his mother at

Dulles International Airport for four hours—a heinous act defended, nonetheless, by the White House, which argued the child posed "a security risk." Or the federal employee who detained a woman and her two small children at Dulles for twenty hours without food. She was handcuffed throughout her detainment, even when she used the bathroom. And then there is the sixty-five-year-old mother on her way to visit her son, a serviceman stationed at Fort Bragg, who was held at Kennedy International Airport for thirty-three hours and denied the use of her wheelchair.[17] These are just three of the multiple victims of Trump's cruelty visited upon children, mothers, and the elderly—implemented by federal employees. The common denominator among those being persecuted by the Trump administration is their lack of white skin and thus white privilege. We imagine those who inflict inhumane suffering on other humans to be guards at Nazi concentration camps or Siberian gulags. But as Hannah Arendt reminds us, banal people—clergy, Boy Scouts, nursing mothers, and cookie-baking grandmas—all have the capacity to engage in evil acts if they believe they are serving a higher purpose.

We would be mistaken to blame only Trump for creating this current barbarous culture of cruelty. His years in office did not initiate a new age within US history but rather they reinforced the historical norm. The birthright whites possess means they get to gorge themselves on fruit from the trees planted by others. The dispossessed cross borders to feed white families. They till the soil, plant the seeds, and harvest the food while whites build fences to prevent laborers from eating what their back-breaking toil has brought forth. Building fences and cages and walls may have its economic advantages, but acquiescence to perverse individual acts and government policies is more than simply the pursuit of economic self-interest. There is an erotic component. Erect walls are never enough to reach the sexual satisfaction sadism satiates. Yes, such acts are brutal and cruel, as the libertine Marquis de Sade reminds us, "It is always by way of pain one arrives at pleasure."[18] A sexual component to the US culture of cruelty has always existed. Doms and dominatrices achieve ecstasy viewing the humiliation and suffering of others. Acts demonstrating supremacy over other provides an orgasmic release. How else can we understand the normalization of raping Black, Brown, Red, and Yellow female bodies throughout US history? Or on occasion, the bodies of men and boys of color? A society claiming faithfulness to Christian virtues legitimized the pleasure of inflicting such pain. The United States was founded on and ruled by a dominating white penis under whose shadow all who are not white have been castrated.

Sexism moves beyond just the oppression of women. Racism, ethnic discrimination, homophobia, transphobia, and classism are not distinct categories operating in isolated compartments. All these manifestations of repression are modeled after sexism, and to fully understand how all these oppressive expressions operate, we must give close attention to sexist-based paradigms, specifically the attempt to domesticate and dominate all who do not have a white penis, be they women of any color or men who are not white. Sexism, as the archetype for all forms of oppression, is as much about racism and classism as it is about gender oppression. Men of color—like all women regardless of color—are created by the ultimate, almighty, well-hung white God to occupy a role inferior to white men. As Mary Daly once quipped, "If God is male, then the male is God."[19] To update Daly's assertion, I would say: "If God is a white male, then the white male is God." Seeing white men as gods means that all who lack a white penis fall short of divinity. All who are of color are not created in the image of a white God, regardless of their gender, and are defined, relegated, and placed in the position to which women have been consigned, defined within a patriarchal structure as passive and submissive, occupying bent-over positions for easy mounting.

White males are endowed by their white creator with the equipment to protect, through domination, all who lack a white penis. They forge history by way of their phallus. Only explorers planting their flagpole upon virgin lands, conquerors subduing and domesticating the untamed wilderness, and winners of the West are true, rugged, self-sufficient men. Their power, privilege, and profits are the result of the ultimate metaphoric sign—the white penis—which is derived by weaving oppression into laws, traditions, customs, and social structures. They self-construct their ego based on an illusory self-definition that negates all who lack white penises for their supposed inability to dominate, subjugate, and domesticate. Because only white men forged civilizations (ignoring those founded by other cultures), everyone else is believed to suffer from penis envy. They are nothing, lacking personhood and subjectivity, because the white man's penis represents a unifying purpose and a reason for existence. Those who are neither white nor male are expected to submerge their identity to the toxic masculinity of whiteness in order to meet white males' libidinous cravings for supremacy. Relegated to the role of passiveness, communities of color—regardless of gender—have historically and continuously been expected to offer themselves up as living sacrifices for the well-being of whites and their endeavors.

The potent significance of the white penis veils the socioeconomic power amassed by those with access to all that the phallus represents. Lacking a white penis means nonexistence, except as designated by the yearnings of those who possess one. Communities of color, who have been castrated and lack the power, privilege, and profit afforded by the phallic symbol, occupy the position where both their bodies and minds are forcefully and violently raped. They are relegated to primitive and exotic spaces to be enjoyed by those who have proven their misogynist authority. Inferiority becomes engraved in the very flesh of those lacking the power of patriarchy, while those claiming possession of a white penis—regardless of gender, for white women can always procure strap-ons—become enslaved to false visions of superiority.

In truth, no one really has a penis. Those lacking a white penis must submerge their true identities to survive, while those relying on their white penises as essential to their identity to survive must live up to a false construction that strips them of their very humanity. Nonwhite men are forcefully deprived of what this culture determines the white penis represents. Those who possess a white penis exist always threatened with possible loss of all it signifies, a loss to be prevented at all cost and by whatever means necessary. Overcompensation, via braggadocious white supremacist rhetoric, masks the reality of supremacism's erectile dysfunction. Violence becomes the Viagra enhancing the ability to perform domination.

The Trump years, and those of whoever follows him into the Oval Office, are products of an obsessive neurotic condition oriented toward the carnal pleasures derived from sadism, a reflection of a Euro-American ethos founded when the first white man set foot upon this hemisphere and gazed upon the naked body of an Indigenous person before raping and killing her. Nationalist Christianity has normalized the orgasmic release experienced in causing pain and humiliation. The future presidents of the Republic may not derive as much erotic pleasure as Trump appears to when he is humiliating his targets, but they will nonetheless participate in the orgy of white supremacy because, thus far, no one who ever sat in the Oval Office seriously reflected upon the sadistic culture of Euro-Americans. As long as cages continue to be built for children, we will all continue to live under the shadow of the white penis.

Building upon Death

Building cages for children, a byproduct of white supremacy, is not only morally indefensible, but it is a symptom of a serious malady. The United States suffers from the mental illness of supremacism. White superiority as a mental affliction, as an infirmity, leads good-intentioned, moral white folk into committing such psychopathic acts as refusing to feel empathy when separating a Brown-skinned five-year-old from his mother and handcuffing him for hours. The contagious and fast-spreading virus of white supremacy makes white people indifferent toward the physical and psychological torture they impose—through their silence and complicity—upon the most vulnerable among us, the least of these. How else can one explain white church folk bending their knees in holy submission to God while simultaneously supporting, through their vote or their silence, placing Brown children in cages? They ignore the Prince of Peace they claim to follow, specifically his warning, "Much better would it be to be thrown into the sea with a millstone tied around their neck than to cause one of these little ones to stumble" (Luke 17:2). Whether this psychopathic disease is learned or inherited is for geneticists and philosophers to debate.

The fever this national ailment causes leads it sufferers to lash out in anger when they feel wronged, as demonstrated by a thin-skinned president's angry daily tweets over the most insignificant slights. According to a 2007 study examining the national, collective narcissism of the in-group (whites), which combined anti-elitism with the belief that they hold a superior vision of what it means to be an American, researchers found that support for Trump correlated with the in-group's unrealistic belief in their greatness, which increased their perceived societal disadvantage caused by out-groups (people of color).[20] Like many suffering from the coronavirus, the nation is feverish, suffering delusions that those who are not real Americans have an unfair advantage due to some past misfortune (slavery) or because they (illegals) are gaming and draining the system. This illness impairs their ability to reason, making them blindly loyal to their messiah. This is a contagious pathogen fogging the minds of those infected, blurring their vision of what is right and wrong, moral and immoral. Constant hand-washing and social distancing are no longer sufficient to contain the virus of superiority. In fact, it's too late, since now the entire population is infected as the Black and Brown body counts rise. Centuries of imposing trauma on nonwhite bodies has altered the DNA of this country, making infliction of pain and torture upon fellow humans the normative *operatio mundi*, preventing white bodies from also experiencing human flourishing.

We see once-intelligent people in the throes of this disease as their immune system is comprised to the point of not only tolerating falsehoods and illusions as the new reality, but joyfully embracing being deceived. Through political lies, white self-preservation is possible. Large swaths of white America are disease-ridden as the supremacist pandemic spreads globally, metamorphosing white Christians who once claimed to lift up Jesus to now lifting up authoritarian despots who mouth family values. Apologist Christians for Trump no longer rely merely on prayer, organizing, and voting. They now embrace the toxic masculine spirit of brown shirts—as demonstrated by Jerry Falwell Jr.'s call to the faithful to resist turning the other cheek in favor of becoming "street fighters." As he tweeted on September 28, 2018, "Conservatives & Christians need to stop electing 'nice guys.' They might make great Christian leaders but the US needs street fighters like @realDonaldTrump at every level of government b/c the liberal fascists Dems are playing for keeps & Repub leaders are a bunch of wimps!" Not wanting to disappoint, when candidate Trump was asked during a radio interview what Bible verse or story most informed his thinking or his character, he responded, after some fumbling, with "an eye for an eye."[21]

Never mind that this verse, found in Exodus 21:23-25, attempts to limit revenge through the concept of *lex talionis*, which restricts penalization for an injury to the same level of intensity as was inflicted upon the injured party. Unbeknownst to Trump, but basic knowledge among Christians, is Jesus's renunciation of this passage as recorded in Matthew 5:38-42, where he teaches that rather than accepting restrained revenge as previously taught—an eye for an eye—believers are to "turn the other cheek." But even if he rejects the good news proclaimed by Jesus Christ, Trump still misses the point of the Hebrew Bible's call to limit retaliation to the same degree as suffered by the injured party. Ignoring both the Hebrew Bible and the New Testament, Trump embraces over-the-top retaliation, or as he put it during an interview on the Fox entertainment show *Hannity* on November 10, 2015, "Anybody who hits me, we're gonna hit them ten times harder."[22]

Once the disease is full blown, humanity—according

to their afflicted minds—is redefined by its inhuman treatments of others. The impertinent, foul white pus discharged from this illness blames everything and everyone except their supremacism. During a podcast hosted by the "bodega boys"—Desus Nice and Kid Mero—they coined a word to describe this impudent disease, *caucacity*: the portmanteau words formed by blending *caucasian* with *audacity*. Whites suffer from this caucacity disease. Caucacity describes the willingness and entitlement to take bold actions or engage in risky behavior to the detriment of others, specifically people of color. Only white people—because society normalizes and legitimates their power, profit, and privilege—feel safe and secure in participating in bold, destructive actions or risky behavior. It does not matter whether, on March 8, 2020, Trump retweeted a picture of himself fiddling like the emperor Nero with the caption, "My next piece is called—Nothing can stop what's coming," because the coronavirus was literally becoming a global pandemic and the stock markets were in the midst of a freefall. All that mattered was that he delivered results to his base by appointing judges in favor of restricting women's reproductive rights, suppressing LGBTQI civil rights, restructuring the judicial system, and creating an apartheid political structure to keep whites in power. Just as important, he unlocked the nation's treasury for pillaging by business associates and friends. For example, the company Rocket Loans, owned and operated

by billionaire Dan Gilbert, a friend and $750 thousand do-
nor to Trump, received a $50 million loan to manage the
expected deluge of small business loan applications from
firms devastated by the coronavirus-triggered economic
collapse.[23] Furthermore, while signing the $500 billion
stimulus bailout program to corporations on March 27,
2020, Trump committed to ignoring the bill's provision of
accountability, stating he would thwart the inspector general's oversight abilities.[24]

Caucacity causes psychopathy, an illness that makes its
sufferers lose their humanity and set out to steal the humanity of those who are nonwhites. However, it is far too
easy to dismiss those suffering from caucacity as monsters
to justify our private, visceral reactions to their atrocities.
Simple good–evil binaries fail us when we recognize oppressors and abusers still have the capacity to pet dogs, kiss
their children, and feel compassion. Monsters are able to
discover their humanity and get saved. Although monsters
are themselves victims of the social structures designed to
privilege them, they remain complicit with said structures and should not be glibly excused. We wonder how
much their monstrousity is a reflection of what they had
to learn so they could belong to what was presented as a
superior and exceptional people. How much of their apathy toward tortured bodies of color is learned behavior
since childhood? Yes, they have grown up to love their own

children, give to charity, go to church, and sing hymns of God's glory. And yet, something malevolent brews within them everyday. Clergy, Boy Scouts, nursing mothers, and cookie-baking grandmas still yell with full gusto, "Build that wall." How can these good, hard-working, dog-petting white folk support politicians who maintain and sustain hatred?

Hatred, as I wrote before, has always been a powerful political tool, creating unity against a common enemy who is different—different because they speak a dissimilar language or have distinctive racial features. They are different because they worship a God who goes by another name. They are different because they celebrate a sexual orientation that moves beyond a fixed gender binary. Teaching people to be suspicious of those who are different fosters their loyalty to despots who vow to keep them safe from differences. Good people hate out of a fear of losing whatever perceived power, profit, or privilege they claim to possess. Fear of "them" taking our jobs, our place, or our women has always been an influential instigator. In his supposed comeback 2020 campaign rally at Tulsa, Trump capitalized on this fear by referring to COVID-19 as the "kung flu," by warning of "tough *hombre* breaking into your home while you are away and your young wife is alone," and by equating the removal of statues glorifying the Confederacy defense of slavery with destroying "our heritage."[25] More chilling than the unapologetic embrace of racism's tropes was how the crowd enthusiastically reacted, riled up by these clear calls to whiteness. The rally, originally scheduled for June 19, took place on June 20. Trump was forced to change the date after pushback concerning his racial insensitivity—but not before claiming "I made Juneteenth very famous."[26]

Hatred, fear, and loathing flourish in times of turmoil when the basic social contract is in tatters, when keeping one's nose to the grindstone fails to lead to any advancement, when the norm is a downward economic spiral in which the rich get wealthier and the middle class poorer, and when children will live a life with fewer opportunities than their parents. During these times, slogans like putting America first (read as white America) become alluring. Those who feel forgotten and lack good-paying jobs need someone to blame. Supporters of whiteness look at those they see as foreigners and accuse them of cutting in line to receive unearned entitlements. Their rage over their predicament is misdirected. Rather than trickling upward toward those who are benefiting from the status quo, their anger gushes downward to those who share their economic plight. History shows that someone is always waiting in the wings who can tap into the frustrations of good people who pet their dogs. The few who benefit from the way society is structured offer those relegated to the underside and who seem to hold back real Americans as a convenient scapegoat to distract good people from their own responsibility for their quandary.

The educationally challenged are not the only ones susceptible to being infected with caucacity. We would be mistaken to assume racism and ethnic discrimination are symptoms of ignorance, infecting those who lack schooling in greater numbers. Educated whites, even those holding PhDs, have falsely assumed bigots were simply unenlightened; therefore, because they are educated, they cannot be racist. But racism is not a product of ignorance or narrow-mindedness that is easily remedied by better education. Education, in this case, is not the answer. According to a comprehensive study that examined data gathered over three decades, the hypothesis that those with higher cognitive abilities were somehow more committed to racial equality and promoted racial tolerance turned out to be a myth. While the more educated did demonstrate a pronounced rejection of overt prejudice undergirded by an abstract and superficial commitment to the idea of racial equality, they nonetheless remained opposed to the most benign policies that could challenge the dominant group's social status. They are no more likely than those with less education to support remedial policies for racial inequality.[27]

The educated may talk the talk, but they, like their skin-folk who suffer from a deficiency of intellectual aptitude, fail to walk the walk. Their education merely facilitates the ability to better rationalize their biases. So, what good is it if some people can intellectually wax poetic about the iniquities of racism if they are just as committed to protecting their unearned profit, privilege, and power as the less educated? They do not overtly express biases or prejudices because they learned how to better mask their racism and complicity through xenophobic structures. These sophisticated racists are more treacherous to communities of color than their less educated, Confederate flag-waving, redneck skinfolk. While people of color can better plan to protect themselves from those who blatantly express race-based stereotypes, they find it more difficult and dangerous to safeguard against courteous racist allies. Is it any wonder people of color do not fully trust their so-called white allies, especially well-educated white allies?

White educated liberals like these honestly believe they are responsible for much of the good done for those who live on the margins of society, never pausing to consider the oppressive pain they consciously or unconsciously systematically and institutionally impose upon the disenfranchised. Overly defensive, they respond indignantly when confronted or held accountable for actions complicit with racist ideology, saying, "I don't have a racist bone in my body"—a sure sign they are racist. I can even hear these deniers of racist complicity wonder aloud about the ungratefulness of people of color who fail to recognize and appreciate all white liberals have done for them! Professor of pedagogy Robin DeAngelo, who made a small fortune repackaging what scholars of color have been saying all along, penned the phrase "white fragility" to describe the common script white people follow when confronted with their race privilege. She elucidates how, when challenged, whites experience "patterns of confusion, defensiveness and righteous indignation. When confronted with a challenge to white racial codes, many white liberals use speech of self-defense. This discourse enables defenders to protect their moral character against what they perceive as accusation and attack while deflecting any recognition of culpability or need of accountability."[28] No doubt the greatest failure of the white liberal church, probably due to its commitment to tolerance (as if racist thought could ever be tolerated), is their refusal to denounce conservative white Christians as heretics; but then again, if they do, wouldn't that be the pot calling the kettle black?

Those who sympathize with white supremacy and suffer the symptoms of caucacity are still able to pet their dogs and hug their grandchildren. They can still note the exquisiteness of a rose and weep at the beauty of an opera. The sins of the father and mother are manifested in their children, making them no different than those who made the trains run on time to deliver the innocent to their demise in places with names like Chelmno, Sobibor, and

Treblinka. What is truly frightening about those infected with caucacity is how normal they appear, like models for a Norman Rockwell portrait, and how they have legitimized their white ethnonationalism. Regardless of how much they profess to be Christians or how fervently they wave the stars and stripes, the illness has made them into brain-eating zombies, only rather than feasting on the brains of others, they devour their own. Their support for policies and politicians that bring death and destruction to those outside their white Christian tribe makes them complicit with crimes against humanity, even if they are banal clergy, Boy Scouts, nursing mothers, or cookie-baking grandmas who pet their dogs. Maybe, in the final analysis, there is no such thing as a dog-petter who is a good person if that person embraces or remains complicit with white supremacy. Not, at least, according to the story of the sheep and the goats.

The Color-Blind Cure

During the 1960s, people of color began to rebel against caucacity in the form of the Black Civil Rights movement, the American Indian movement, and El Movimiento. Progress was made to create a more perfect union, a nation where individuals do not advance due to their white skin pigmentation but through their abilities. These progressive movements began chipping away at the foundations of white privilege, threatening white supremacy. And while they did not achieve a level playing field, they made some advances, such as voting rights and equal housing opportunities, especially when compared to the earlier Jim and Jane Crow years in the South or the Juan or Juana Cuervo años in the Southwest. Still, despite these advances, Euro-Americans continued to disproportionately hold the more desirable jobs and attend the most prestigious educational institutions. The browning of America and the endangerment of white affirmative action gave rise to a white identity crisis. "This is no longer my country!" "I no longer recognize my country!" "I must take my country back!" These battle cries, amplified by demagogues and religious leaders, demanded action. In response, a kinder and gentler form of oppression was made possible by adopting and implementing political correctness. Progressives could gently guide marginalized groups to less-threatening ways of confronting their subjugation. Suffering from racial ignorance, these liberal whites held strong opinions on race relationships but had little if any empirical knowledge about their own ignorance on the subject. Polite racism became the established norm—until the rise of Trump.

Unwilling to vanquish white supremacy or challenge neoliberalism, whites chose to advocate an alleged color blindness as the cure for caucacity, a litmus test that appears progressive while maintaining supremacism. Of course, most whites would never be so foolish as to voice blatantly racist comments or appear to violate the rules of political correctness, at least not in the presence of people of color. Nevertheless, wishing to preserve white advantages through the denial of racial differences led them to advocate color blindness, a placebo that had no effect on caucacity. Many well-meaning whites tell themselves, "I don't see color. Like Martin Luther King Jr., I do not judge people by the color of their skin but by the content of their character. I treat everyone the same!" Thus they declare race is meaningless. But as many people of color know all too well, race divisions are a daily experience negatively influencing every aspect of life. But even if we accept the myth that an individual does not see color, social structures are designed to see color for them and act accordingly. Calling for a color-blind society to establish a level playing field, whites mask their resentment of the present economic crises. Many blame the crises on so-called "unfair advantages" given to nonwhites, which can only be mediated when everyone is supposedly treated in the same way, ignoring how social structures continue to privilege whites in spite of whites' outspoken claims concerning color blindness.

Pretending they cannot see color, white Christianity proclaims their white Jesus as Lord of all. They seek racial harmony and reconciliation through a personal relationship with their white Jesus who, they claim, can move across racial and ethnic lines. All who make the white Jesus their Lord become brothers and sisters, regardless of their race or ethnicity, as those of color assimilate into whiteness. Personal piety over and against societal changes provides a false sense of righteousness that never needs to examine its complicity with racist structures. Such arguments, wishing to preserve white advantages through the denial of racial differences, damn any hope of liberation among the marginalized. Those who offer reconciliatory rhetoric while remaining determined not to forsake any of the benefits associated with whiteness can never be allowed to define the terms of racial reconciliation; that duty, instead, must fall on the shoulders of those occupying the underside of society, those yearning for justice. Their struggle for a more just social order becomes the grassroots context from which any meaningful discussion of reconciliation must arise, a reconciliation based on the pursuit of salvation and liberation.

No doubt white people can experience the vicissitudes of life—bankruptcy, layoff, financial reversal, coronavirus infection, or poverty, to name but a few possibilities. But they will never face daily, institutionalized racism or ethnic discrimination that negatively impacts every aspect of their existence, leading to a race-based stress that is manifested as lower economic success and shorter life expectancy. When whites experience economic downward mobility, they are encouraged to blame people of color for their descending slide by the top 1 percent skinfolk who benefit the most by the reorganizing of the economic system. A rigged system prevents the white middle class from economically succeeding and joining the 1 percent. To their minds, these structures are rigged against hard-working Americans—white Americans. Why can't everyone be treated the same, whites wonder—ignorant of how social structures have been historically designed to benefit them. If everyone were treated the same, maybe then the white middle class could have a fighting chance to succeed. Color blindness becomes the racist solution. Claiming color blindness comforts whites who see themselves as progressive on issues concerning race and ethnicity. Since they see themselves as good people holding strong Christian values, they find the notion that they are racist inconceivable, because racists are evil people who wear hoods and burn crosses. Because they neither cry out *Seig heil* nor use racial slurs (singing the N-word in certain songs doesn't count), they cannot, therefore, be racist.

Missing from the equation is the realization that racism has nothing to do with belief. Racism and ethnic discrimination are neither individual prejudices nor biases but are the institutionalization of uneven power relationships based on ethnicity or skin pigmentation. It does not matter if everyone does not hold prejudiced or biased views. It does not matter if white people marched with Martin Luther King Jr. or voted for Barack Obama. Taking a critical race theory class in college is insufficient. Having a Black friend or engaging in a close relationship with a Latinx does not make the white person an authority on the subject of racism. White people (and here I specifically mean those with white skin pigmentation) have been taught to be racist since birth. Also, they have been taught to be blind to their racism. In effect, they are indeed racist, even if they are recovering racists, because regardless of their beliefs, society is carefully constructed to be racist on their behalf. In this same way, all cisgender males (myself included) are recovering sexists. My belief in women's equality or their right to wear pink pussy hats at rallies (white women's rallies, because women of color would require different color hats) makes no difference to my complicity with sexist structures. Since the day I was born with a penis, all of society has been designed and exists to provide me with unearned privileges, profits, and power over cisgender women (as well as the queer community), even though I remain subjected to white penises. I am attempting to take intentional steps toward recovery from sexism, but I have to live within a vast and powerful system that negates these intentions—no matter how good they might be. Likewise, while some white people might be attempting to recover from racism, they are nevertheless living within a vast and powerful system built to negate these attempts.

What I need is praxis designed to use the power I have

been afforded by my gender to dismantle the very sexist structures responsible for providing me with said power, not tears of guilt or words of self-flagellation. If communities of color are even remotely right in their assessment concerning white people's unexamined racism, then maybe whites aren't the good people they imagined themselves to be. It's just easier to simply move on to other topics or just "try to get along" instead of exploring the possibilities of complicity with racist social structures, because the assertion of white complicity with institutionalized racism questions the very moral fabric of these self-deceived good people. We can't simply get along or move on. Communities of color are refusing to quietly go into the night as they occupy streets throughout the nation after the murder of George Floyd. But peaceful protests provide whites with the excuse to become more aggressive, to move beyond the political correctness of color blindness. With the ushering in of the Trump administration, a radical racist neoorthodoxy emerged, amplifying earlier calls for race wars. The racist structures built at the start of the second decade of the new millennium will prove to be more life threatening than any that came before. Communities of color find themselves at the threshold of a new, more dangerous way of being.

4

Revealing Revelations

If 1969 gave us the summer of love, then fifty years later—2019—will most likely be remembered as the year that ushered in a new decade when fear and hatred were crystalized—fear of communities of color, fear of economic distress, and fear of the possible loss of white affirmative action as the potential for a new economic order began to take shape. These fears were soon joined by fear of the coronavirus. As we know from our history, such fears make the US susceptible to political manipulation as hatred of change morphs into hatred of the other. Long after the threat of the coronavirus dissipates and the economy rebounds, the emotional scars upon the nation's ethos will remain. The country can give in to fear and hatred, or it can rise to the occasion by bringing forth a more perfect union. As a nation, we can move toward curing what has historically ailed this country or continue ignoring the sickness laying the nation-body to waste. In the aftermath of the COVID-19 tragedy, can we dare hope for healing? Healing cannot come while white rage remains concealed behind biblical justification for oppressive and repressive social, political, and economic structures. A clear example of white rage was manifested by the political revanchism exhibited during the failed 2020 impeachment trial of President Donald Trump. Prior to the coronavirus outbreak, the January Senate impeachment trial solidified white America in their anger and animosity. This white rage, coupled with the fear of a microscopic viral threat, has led us as a country to the threshold of a new decade that, if current trends continue, will be devastating, especially for communities of color within this country as well as inhabitants throughout the Global South. If Christianity hopes to be a crucial conversation partner as we dream of a new world and a new way of being, then the tenets of nationalist Christianity need to be slain. Specifically, we need to repudiate manipulation of the biblical text to justify systematic oppressive structures.

As the 2010s came to a close, probably the most dangerous biblical interpretation of the latter part of the decade was the celebration of Donald Trump as some modern-day King Cyrus. Nationalist Christians were quick to associate Trump with the sixth-century BCE ruler. King Cyrus was a "pagan" monarch who founded the first Persian empire, the largest domain ever established up to that time. He made Persia great. According to the biblical text, he was unwittingly used by God according to God's purposes. In Isaiah 45:1, God chose Cyrus to accomplish a divine task, unbeknownst to him, to return Jews to the promised land after their exile in Babylon. This non-Jew was proclaimed by the prophet Isaiah to be a *messiah*, the Hebrew word for anointed. For almost sixty years, the middle- and upper-class Jewish population had been estranged from their homeland, deported to Babylon in 597 BCE by King Nebuchadrezzar II (2 Kings 24:14). The Babylonian empire was conquered by King Cyrus in 539 BCE; the following year he issued an edict ending the captivity and piloting a return to Zion to be led by Sheshbazzar (Ezra 1:1–8). Although the First Temple was destroyed by the Babylonians, King Cyrus called for its rebuilding, returning all the vessels that had been carried off (Ezra 1:7–11). Cyrus may have been heralded as a messiah, but he still presided over conquests and massacres. One notable sadistic act included burning alive fourteen young Lydian boys on a funeral pyre as a test of their gods to see if they would be delivered.[1] Why does white Christianity insist on portraying Trump as a modern-day Cyrus? Comparing Trump to Cyrus permits them to overlook biblical principles concerning virtues in favor of political expedience. While previous US presidents had been judged publicly and quite harshly for their moral shortcomings (for instance, Bill Clinton's extramarital affairs), evangelicals today have abandoned such piety litmus tests. One need not be devoted to God or to morality to be used by God. The modern-day Cyrus connection provides white Christians with the necessary cover to excuse how the advocates of family values can unquestionably support an adulterer, a swindler (Trump University), a instigator of political cruelty, and a habitual liar. God chooses imperfect humans to accomplish God's will, they say.

The Evangelicals for Trump political rally of January 3, 2020, which was held in a church, was hastily assembled as needed damage control for a scathing editorial about Trump in *Christianity Today* written by its then-editor Mark Galli. Several evangelical leaders gathered at the seven-thousand-seat sanctuary in Miami to lay hands on and anoint Trump. A self-proclaimed apostle, Guillermo Maldonado, prayed that Trump would fulfill his calling as the new King Cyrus. This wolf in sheep's clothing cried out, "Father, we give you the praise and honor and we ask you that [Trump] can be the Cyrus to bring reaffirmation, to bring change into this nation, and all the nations of the Earth will say America is the greatest nation of the Earth."[2]

Profit can be gained in anointing Trump as King Cyrus. Lance Wallnau, a business consultant and self-proclaimed doctor in ministry who received his degree from an Arizona

PO box, was the first to make the Cyrus-Trump link after claiming God spoke to him, instructing him to compare the forty-fifth president with Isaiah 45. "Donald Trump," he bragged, "is a wrecking ball to the spirit of political correctness."[3] Seeking to cash in on God's voice, he minted "prayer coins," which he sells for $45 each. The coin contains two heads on one side: in the background is a portrait of King Cyrus and in the foreground is the ominous profile of Trump. Even Israel's prime minister, Benjamin Netanyahu, seeing that political gain could be obtained by stroking Trump's fragile ego, made the Cyrus-Trump comparison in March 2018.[4] On the heels of Trump's announcement of moving the US embassy to Jerusalem, Netanyahu said, "I want to tell you that the Jewish people have a long memory, so we remember the proclamation of the great king, Cyrus the Great, a Persian king 2,500 years ago. He proclaimed that the Jewish exiles in Babylon could come back and rebuild our Temple in Jerusalem."[5]

There is no question King Cyrus was a talented ruler, for he was seen at the time as a benevolent despot. He ruled over a well-run government that respected the religious beliefs of all the different groups within the empire, a far cry from the botched-up presidency of Donald Trump. Comparing King Donald to King Cyrus has little to do with biblical prophecy and more to do with claiming a moral and spiritual superiority in justifying support for a moral and spiritual degenerate.

If a biblical figure is needed to which we can compare Trump, probably King Cyrus is not the best archetype. A better choice would be the antichrist of the Book of Revelation.

The Rise of Antichrists

US nationalist Christians saw this nation through apocalyptic eyes. Proclaiming themselves the light of Christ, these Christians' nation-building efforts would supposedly have global and eternal significance. The rise of the United States would literally usher in the second coming of Christ. Prior to the Civil War, most Christians embraced postmillennialism (a thousand-year golden age of peace *before* Christ returns). They believed the only thing preventing the second coming of Christ was the incessant sin of slavery. Once slavery was abolished, the golden age could commence within the United States. This religious fervor led many to join the abolitionist movement. But with the bloody drudgery of a civil war dividing families, followed by the chaos and carnage wrought by the South's opposition to Reconstruction, the optimism and hopefulness of postmillennialism gave way to disappointment in human nature. Society was deemed incapable of bringing forth a golden age of peace. According to historian George Marsden, dispensationalism with its premillennialist bent (a thousand-year golden age of peace *after* Christ returns) gained popularity in the aftermath of what Southerners insisted on calling the War Between the States.[6]

Dispensationalism was a fanciful invention of John Nelson Darby in the 1870s. He divided human history into seven dispensations: (1) Innocence (prior to the fall); (2) Conscience (from the fall up to the Flood); (3) Human Government (from the Flood to the call of Abraham); (4) Promise (from the call of Abraham to the giving of the law at Mount Sinai); (5) Law (from the giving of the law to the death of Christ); (6) Grace (from the giving of the Spirit at Pentecost to Christ's second coming); and (7) Kingdom (from the second coming of Christ to the establishment of the throne of judgment). This division of human history became popular with evangelicals such as D. L. Moody and C. I. Scofield, who blended dispensationalist dogmas to create a manifestation of white Christianity that is conservative, fundamentalist, and evangelical. Followers of this peculiar form of white Christianity were suspicious of the Social Gospel, justice work, and humanitarian initiatives. They viewed those who challenged oppressive social structures like racism, misogyny, xenophobia, or classism as attempting to create a thousand-year golden age of peace *without* Christ. Working for a more just social system was viewed as the faux activities of the devil or as endeavors masquerading as socialism. Because we are saved by grace alone, not works, lest anyone should boast, attempts to practice the good news preached by Jesus in the Sermon of the Mount were perceived as apostasy. The Golden Rule was for the last dispensation when Christians will reside in Christ's kingdom, not for this current dispensation of grace. The task of creating a society that attends to the hungry, the thirsty, and the naked has no place in white Christianity.

One contribution dispensationalists made to white Christian discourse is the concept of an antichrist, an actual human of flesh-and-blood who becomes the cosmic nemesis of Jesus. Probably no other person in recent times has contributed more ink to the antichrist fantasy than the popular author Hal Lindsey, who with his 1970 national best-seller *The Late Great Planet Earth* sought to match current events with biblical prophecy. Claiming to read the signs of the times, he mapped out how by the next decade the earth would implode, an antichrist would arise, and the white Jesus would return around 1988.[7] In 1976 the book was adapted into a film narrated by Orson Wells, and by 1990 the book had sold over twenty-eight million copies. Our understanding today of the antichrist has more to do with Lindsey's imagination than with any other cultural influence. As the second coming became more imminent, he wrote another book in 1981 titled *The 1980's: Countdown to Armageddon*, claiming "the decade of the 1980s could very well be the last decade of history as we know it."[8] When the world didn't end in the 1980s, white people's understanding of the antichrist required an update. The extremely popular twelve-book Left Behind series written by Tim LaHaye and Jerry Jenkins, especially the third book of the series titled *Nicolae*, provided the antichrist a much-needed facelift. Although their stories were fictional, the authors insisted their version of future events was correctly based on the only possible valid and literal interpretation of the biblical text. Making its debut in 1995, the series had sold over eighty million books by 2006.

These modern-day biblical charlatans spun a tale about how they envision the end of time. True believers—predominately white Christians—will first be raptured, a belief based on 1 Thessalonians 4:15–18, which describes how Christ will return and take up into the clouds the believers, along with those being resurrected from the dead. Those remaining on planet earth—mainly multiculturalists, feminists, queers, non-Christians, secularists, and liberals—become enemies of Christ. They will face seven years of tribulation, a period marked by global trial and suffering. During the tribulation, the antichrist will arise and establish a world-wide government. Under the antichrist's rule, hell literally breaks loose. This antichrist is eventually assassinated, but on the third day rises from the dead, indwelt by Satan. Total allegiance to the antichrist is demanded, and those who refuse are sent to guillotines erected in public squares throughout the world. Eventually, the antichrist enters the rebuilt Temple in Jerusalem and declares himself god. His end comes when he gathers the world's armies for a cosmic battle at the fields of Armageddon against Christ, who returns riding a white horse to wreak bloody havoc on the unfaithful.

An Antichrist for Our Times

Let's be clear, Trump is not the antichrist of the dispensationalist imagination who will usher in the final cosmic battle at Armageddon. When the author of the book of Revelation described the antichrist (13:1–10), he did not offer a prophesy to be deciphered by biblical sleuths some two thousand years later so they could make millions of dollars outing the one person who will accompany the final destruction of planet earth. When Revelation was written, Nero—emperor of Rome—best personified the antichrist. Readers of the time had no difficulty understanding the coded language chosen by the Patmos author to conceal the antichrist's identity. If the writer had been less discreet and more direct, then surely they would have faced imperial retribution. Revelation was written to comfort a hurting church facing persecution and loss. The writer was not some Nostradamus writing in riddles and planting clues about future events, which could then be continuously re-interpreted to fit whatever arbitrary events occurred in the future. Such prophetic pronouncements would have made no sense to the persecuted church in desperate need of a pastoral word concerning their world, their "now." Revelation met the specific need of that ancient church. And yet, the text took on greater significance than just a word for a particular time, warning future generations of believers that they too might face political leaders who would arise claiming divinity and engaging in battle with those who chose to live a life seeking to implement the teachings of Jesus Christ. There is not just one antichrist—Nero—but many like him who will arise throughout history.

Nero would neither be the first nor the last antichrist to arise. Every generation has its Nero, its antichrist. Trump is but one of thousands throughout history who fit the description of what is an antichrist. And yet, one is left dumbfounded by how those who faithfully chart current events to see how they are being fulfilled through the enigmatic lens of biblical prophecies are totally missing the presence of the antichrist for this generation. Trump resonates with how the antichrist was envisioned and described by Lindsey, LaHaye, and Jenkins. He and so many other antichrists throughout history share certain common denominators as expounded by dispensationalist Christians. Trump is definitely no King Cyrus, but he surely fits the description of an antichrist. According to the interpretations of dispensationalists, this antichrist can best be described as

◆ One whose "conquest will be rapid . . . [who will] be very strong and powerful . . . self-assured and proud"⁹

From obscurity, a literal political joke rapidly rose to become the most powerful man on the planet. His rapid rise to power was partly based on promising safety and security from the fear and distrust he stirred up—a textbook maneuver employed by caudillos everywhere. As a half-truth huckster, Trump paints a portrait in which the United States is doing great under his stewardship—Keep America Great—but is threatened nonetheless by both external forces (hordes of Brown people and Muslim terrorists) and internal forces (Democrats, liberals, and socialists). Playing on the anxieties of white Christian conservatives, he elicits knee-jerk responses.

As long as Latinxs are portrayed as invading Brown hordes out to kill and destroy Euro-Americans' way of life—conservative brains seem to be wired to embrace saviors pointing out the threat and offering protection. "Only I can fix it,"¹⁰ a self-assured and proud Trump promised during the 2016 Republican Convention, and conservatives have since maintained that indeed only he can. Belief in saviors outweighs crude and brutish character traits of autocrats rapidly rising in politics. Constant fearmongering, according to a 2006 study, pushes individuals toward more conservative, nationalistic views. Existential fear increases support for extreme military actions, which could lead to the death of thousands of civilians.[11] This fear of the Brown menace normalizes concentration camps as a necessary evil in the heroic epic battle against those who are the objects of fear. Self-assured and proud antichrists, then and now, who present themselves as strong and powerful saviors against the fear they instigated among the people, rapidly rise through concentration of power.

◆ *One who rises as a result of chaos*

During Trump's 2017 inaugural address, he presented himself as a savior declaring "American carnage stops right here and stops right now."[12] It does not matter that no economic, political, or social indicators existed documenting this supposed carnage. The id-based rallies that followed solidified fawning devotees regardless of his ability to be footloose with facts. Trump simply needed to say carnage existed, and many of the uninformed and ill-informed, unaware of how much they simply do not know, believed him. Likewise, in July 2020, all he needed to say was that the coronavirus would simply disappear, claiming the number of infections were decreasing, for diehard believers to believe, even though 2.7 million tested positive and 130,000 died.[13] When science or independent investigative news sources presents data contrary to Trump's cosmology, Trumpites, whose worldview is shaped by religious pretenders and Fox News pundits, are encouraged to dismiss facts as hoax. The unsubstantiated carnage and chaos envisioned in 2017 are accepted as truth while the carnage and chaos of 2020 are downplayed and dismissed. Maybe the carnage to which Trump referred in 2017 was the election of a Black man to the highest office eight years earlier. If so, this straw that broke the camel's back unleashed a whitelash that caused the mask of political correctness, poorly concealing white supremacists' faces, to slip. Make America White Again sought remedies from a previously unresponsive government to correct and revenge the so-called "carnage and chaos" caused by the perceived loss of white affirmative action.

Ignoring reality, the many Euro-Americans who voted for Trump felt satisfied after having felt abandoned by their nation. Many professed after the election that they voted "to make a point"—to flip a bird at DC—to raise an offensive middle finger toward a government led by a Black man. For some whites who claim rugged individualism, there is an attraction in welcoming a different form of chaos than the one used to motivate credulous minds. Fearing the carnage Trump exploits to garner votes, they find security and pleasure in exerting their own form of carnage. Antichrists, not surprisingly, attract like-minded trolls with schadenfreude fixations. Trump's use of demeaning, childish, and bullying phrases such as "Little Marco," "Lying Ted," "Crooked Hillary," and the more racist "Pocahontas," not only entertains his base but secures votes from those who appreciate a president "who speaks his mind."

♦ *One "able to mesmerize an audience"*

Reducing politics to mesmerizing the audience for the purpose of entertainment is one of the traits that marks an antichrist.[14] In a neuroanalytical study conducted by Spark Neuro, which measured emotion and attention to assist advertisers in optimizing their message, subjects were exposed to forty minutes of presidential debates and commercials from 2016. The data obtained for this research were gathered via galvanic skin responses, electroencephalograms, eye-tracking, microfacial recognition, and the subject's level of emotional response. Regardless of those who protested that they did not like Trump's Islamophobic or racist assertions, his commentary, according to the brainwave studies, held the subjects' attention at a level seven in a ten-point-scale, better than the most popular television commercials at the time. By comparison, Hillary Clinton—his presidential opponent—averaged four points out of the ten-point-scale, signifying boredom.[15] This measured amount of mental energy involved in focusing on a particular subject, known as cathexis, upon Trump and his bluster, was a powerful indicator of white devotion and apostasy.

White Christians, but especially white evangelicals, continue to be mesmerized by this megalomaniac reality-television star, who with bloviating speeches and pugnacious tweets remains incandescent for all the wrong reasons. According to a 2020 survey that measured the time prior to Trump's becoming the official nominee of the Republican Party, his popularity never reached a majority among white evangelicals. But between the time of his nomination and that of his inauguration, his favorability among white evangelicals shot up beyond the 60 percent mark. Following his inauguration, his favorability among white evangelicals has remained between 65 and 77 percent with an average of 71 percent. Among the 77 percent who approve of his job performance, 40 percent say there is almost nothing Trump can do to lose their support. However, among the general public, Trump has been unable to increase his favorability numbers above the low 40 percent.[16]

A few religious leaders have seen the danger of an evangelical audience worshiping the golden calf. Mark Galli, as then-editor of *Christianity Today*, attempted to shake his fellow evangelicals from their idolatrous stupor, writing a scathing 2019 editorial that warned that the president is "morally lost and confused" and that his actions are "profoundly immoral." In addition, Galli referenced the numerous political appointees Trump made who have now become convicted criminals. Trump, according to the editorial, "has

dumbed down the idea of morality in his administration."
And what about the King Cyrus angle? According to Galli,
"None of the president's positives [*sic*] can balance the moral
and political danger we face under a leader of such grossly
immoral character."[17]

John Grano and Richard Land fired back with a rebuttal
published in *The Christian Post*. To them, Galli's piece was
"disdainful, dismissive, [and an] elitist posture toward their
fellow Christians [that] may well do far more long-term
damage to American Christianity and its witness than any
current prudential support for President Trump will ever
cause."[18] Sadly Grano and Land are wrong. The greatest
long-term damage is the normative continuation of their—
and the greater evangelical community's—unchecked white
privilege, which is currently mesmerized by the antichrist
of this particular moment in time.

◆ *One who is allied with Gog—Russia*

Among apocalyptic aficionados, ancient Gog has been
identified as modern Russia, not due to any archaeological evidence or DNA analysis, but simply because such
a connection supports their imaginary metanarrative.[19]
Whether it be the Soviet Union during Lindsey's time or
the Russia of today, the link has more to do with the psyche
of most Euro-Americans than with any facts. Russia, for

over a century, has been the major adversary of the United States, what Reagan once called the "evil empire." The Soviet Union's "evilness" was due to its anti-capitalist, atheistic economic and religious structures, the perfect nemesis for the United States. But with the demise of the Soviet Union, this animosity has softened among nationalist Christians, who have become fascinated by countries with autocratic, nondemocratic rule.

Even though many whites embraced color blindness as a way to dismiss the existence of racism as a reality, foreign adversaries like Russia not only fully acknowledge the authenticity of racism's existence in the US but have successfully manipulated this dysfunctionality to inflame and exacerbate US racial tensions. During the 2016 election, operatives of Russia's external intelligence agency, SVR, created fake Black Lives Matter social media accounts to spread misinformation in an effort to suppress the Black vote, with the intended aim of assisting Trump's candidacy. This foreign attack on the US electoral system was well documented in a report by former counsel for the US Department of Justice Robert Mueller, what Trump and his allies called a "Russian hoax." Shortly after the heavily redacted special counsel's report was released by the Justice Department, Trump discussed this so-called "Russian hoax" with Vladimir Putin by phone for about an hour. Rather than warning his counterpart about not meddling in the next presidential election, Trump shared a smile with Putin, saying something to the effect that Mueller's investigation started up as a mountain and ended up as a mouse.[20]

Undercutting the conclusion of US intelligence agencies that Russia did influence the 2016 election, the Trump administration refused to seriously consider the alerts raised by officials and senior leaders of the Department of Homeland Security concerning the 2020 election. It was "like pulling teeth," according to one official, probably because White House senior staff were reluctant to bring up any issues related to Russia.[21] It has appeared as though the US keeps its fingers in its ears while screaming "No Russian Collusion" as a way to drown out the fact that Russia was stepping up their game. In 2020, the US intelligence community believed Russia had set up troll farms in Nigeria and Ghana in order to influence the 2020 presidential election by inflaming white supremacy groups to incite violence. One US neo-Nazi organization has been shown not only to have ties to Russia but also to benefit from their financial assistance. Russia and/or its oligarchs have for some time been funding far-right groups throughout Europe. The hope was that acts of racial violence here in the US could bolster Trump's reelection bid as conservatives stressed the need for so-called "law and order."[22]

Ironically, that which foreign powers know to be true about us and successfully use to push our red buttons to speed up our own self-destruction, the conservative members of the US population nevertheless pretend does not exist or dismiss as a liberal hoax contrived to spread dissension. The mere fact that the Mueller report clearly showed Russia employed fake social media to provide support to Trump's electoral chances in 2016 indicates that some factions within our midst maintain an alliance with Russia, either willingly or unwittily. If we were to suspend academic rigor and instead accept Russia as ancient Gog (though no archaeological evidence exists making such a link), then probably no modern president since Franklin Delano Roosevelt (who allied the US with the USSR during the Second World War) has provided more support to Gog than Trump, an alliance which, in light of our nation's history, is difficult to understand. This puzzling support for Gog is evident in the White House's silence when it became public in late June 2020 that Russia had been paying bounties to Taliban militants to kill US troops ($100,000 per kill), an assertion made by the US intelligence service in February of that same year in the president's daily brief. And yet, it was ignored by Trump.[23] Rather than holding Russia accountable for facilitating the killing of American troops, Trump instead worked overtime to reinstate Russia in the now G7 after its expulsion for invading and annexing Crimea in 2014.

♦ One who "will deify himself . . . speaking arrogant words and blasphemies" and who is worshiped by all those whose names do not appear in the book of life

Over seven thousand "supporters of faith," many wearing their MAGA red caps, showed up on January 3, 2020, at the International *El Rey Jesús*, a Hispanic evangelical mega-church in Miami, to worship *el rey* Donald, who, rather than claiming he was standing with God, announced, "I really believe we have God on our side."[24] In other words, God makes a preferential option for Trump. Throughout Christian history, the faithful have always been warned about following those who declare themselves gods or whose disciples follow as if they were gods. No greater act of apostasy can occur than proclaiming the Prince of Lies to be the God of Truth. And yet, Trump's devotees, who claim to profess faith in the Almighty, do not challenge his statements.

The greatest blasphemy that can ever come from a Christian's lips is the claim of divinity. Consider the non-Jewish conservative and conspiracy theorist radio host Wayne Allyn Root, who declared Trump to be "King of the Jews," claiming Trump is loved by Jews "like he is the second coming of God." Acknowledging these claims of his divinity, Trump retweeted the blasphemous sycophantic's missive on August 21, 2019. He went on to claim later in the day, "I am the chosen one" (another messianic term).[25] Obviously, when dullards claim Trump's divinity, such hubris can and should easily be ignored. But when the president of the United States of America accepts and promotes this claim, the nation should tremble. The blasphemous ranting that

Trump is the savior of the Jews is not limited to crackpot preachers. Secretary of State and evangelical Mike Pompeo proclaimed on March 21, 2019, that "it's possible [Trump had been sent] to help save the Jewish people."[26] Former secretary of energy, former governor of Texas, and former presidential candidate Rick Perry, during a November 24, 2019, interview aired on Trump's favorite television show, *Fox & Friends*, claimed Trump is "the chosen one" who was sent by God to rule America.[27] Not only is Trump portrayed as "the chosen," but another political leader, Brad Parscale, who serves as his campaign manager, tweeted on April 30 of that same year that "only God could deliver such a savior to our nation." Trump's former press secretary, Sarah Huckabee Sanders, claimed to know the mind of God when she stated months earlier on January 30 that God "wanted Trump to become president."[28]

Probably the greatest demonstration of arrogance a Christian can ever utter is to say that the life of an individual is greater than that of Jesus. Not only was Trump, like Jesus, being crucified by his enemies during the House impeachment inquiry, but it also seems that Jesus had a fairer trial. Speaking during the House impeachment probe, Representative Barry Loudermilk (R-GA) declared, "During [Jesus's] sham trial, Pontius Pilate afforded more rights to Jesus than Democrats have afforded this president in this process." Fred Keller (R-PA) took the holier-than-thou higher road while equating Trump's plight with Jesus's crucifixion, stating, "So I want Democrats voting for impeachment today to know that I'll be praying for them. From the Gospel of Luke, the 23rd chapter, verse 34: 'And Jesus said, "Father, forgive them, for they know not what they do."'"[29] Anyone with an elementary understanding of Christian language knows that terms like "King of the Jews," "the Chosen One," "Savior to the Jews," or just "Savior" are titles exclusively used when referring to Jesus Christ. As irreverent as such comments are when used about anyone else, the true blasphemy, more so than claims or illusions of divinity, is the choice white Christians, specifically evangelicals, have made for political power over and against the rhetoric of the Christian values they once claimed was their reason for rejecting former presidents Obama and Clinton.

This deification of Trump has certainly pleased him and supported his arrogance. As Category 5 Hurricane Dorian threatened the US East Coast in 2019, Trump misspoke, claiming Alabama was at risk. This state was never in any danger, a simple error needing a quick correction lest the wrong information about an approaching deadly natural disaster cost innocent lives. But rather than setting the record straight, Trump could not handle being wrong in public, so like a third-grader caught in an exaggeration, he took a Sharpie pen and altered official government maps to show the storm was bearing down on Alabama.

Messiahs sent by God are incapable of revealing their mistake-prone humanity. This explains why Trump felt he had nothing to ask God to forgive.[30] Therefore, when he got caught falsifying government maps, this would normally have been nothing more than a joke, a laughing matter to be exploited by late-night television talk-show hosts. Unfortunately, the incident lost its humor when the full power of the presidential office was energized to bend truth to Trump's will. The scientific community at the apolitical National Oceanic and Atmospheric Administration (NOAA) was forced to issue a statement, contrary to fact, supporting Trump's error and warning Alabama of a possible threat. Neil Jacobs, the head of NOAA, supported the administration's error only after his employment was threatened.[31] Even the weather must bend to the will of antichrists.

- *One who will suffer "a mortal head wound. . . . He is going to be distinguished as supernatural"*

According to the imagination of tribulationists, the antichrist is praised for having supernatural powers.[32] One such power is the ability to heal. Pastor Hank Kunneman hinted that Trump possessed such powers because he was chosen by God. Kunneman, along with his wife Brenda, have authored several books and together host an internationally televised weekly program. As the coronavirus virus was spreading during the first quarter of 2020, the good pastor reassured the public that America would be spared because Trump is president. Speaking for God, Kunneman prophesied, "Listen to the words that I speak to you at this moment, says the living God. Why do you fear, United States? For I have spoken to you before I will speak to you again, I have extended and opened a window of mercy to this nation at this time. Therefore, the virus that they speak of, the bright prognostication, the diagnosis, the fear, my mercy is the quarantine that shall be greater than what they have spoken to you, United States. . . . And because of the administration that stands in this land, who honor me, who honor the covenants of your forefathers and of the Constitution. And because they have aligned themselves with Israel and because they have sided on the right side of life—life in the womb, life given outside of the womb—there I give life to this nation and I give mercy. . . . Do not fear. The virus is the spirit of God."[33] According to Kunneman, trusting in God and Trump is the best quarantine for the United States. Guillermo Maldonado, the pastor who hosted the Trump rally at his Miami church on January 3, 2020, told his parishioners that fears of COVID-19 could be attributed to a "demonic spirit." He encouraged his congregation to attend Sunday service and ignore official pleas to avoid crowded spaces: "Do you believe God would bring his people to his house to be contagious with the virus? Of course not."[34]

If Trump and God are the saviors from the pandemic, then who is to blame? According to Reverend Ralph Drollinger, who leads weekly Bible studies for the members of Trump's cabinet, America "is experiencing the coronavirus wrath of God." On his Capitol Ministries blog for March 21, 2020,[35] he wrote that people with "depraved minds" had ignited "God's wrath," people like environmentalists and those with "a proclivity toward lesbianism and homosexuality." Secretaries Mike Pompeo, Ben Carson, Betsy DeVos, and Alex Azar attend Drollinger's Wednesday morning Bible studies, yet none have condemned or distanced themselves from his remarks. More disturbing is that Alex Azar, as health secretary, is a prominent member of the White House's coronavirus task force.[36]

Following the president's early denial, mistrust, and blame regarding the growing deadly pandemic, religious leaders devotedly followed the president's lead in merging ignorance with faith. Unfortunately for them, personal piety remains an asinine shield against the scientific realities of the coronavirus. Because of these delays, misdirections, and contradictions regarding the severity of the pandemic, the Trump administration is responsible for much of the rapid spread of COVID-19 within the United States. While no political leaders can be judged for the outbreak of a pandemic, they can be held responsible for the nation's response. Obviously, no matter how well rehearsed a government might be when confronting a global emergency like a plague, mistakes do happen and human error can come into play. Still, when asked during a Rose Garden press conference if he took any responsibility for the lag in making necessary coronavirus testing available, he responded with, "No, I don't take responsibility at all."[37] The buck definitely stops elsewhere in the Trump administration. And yet early on during the pandemic, Trump criticized China's early response to the spread of the virus in Wuhan.[38] Trump and his followers chose to ignore and minimize the ominous classified warnings issued by US intelligence agencies throughout January and February of 2020.[39] Some senators (including Richard Burr, Kelly Loeffler, Diane Feinstein, and Jim Inhofe) took the warnings seriously. Shortly after an intelligence report briefing, and in violation of the 2012 Stock Act, they sold their stock portfolios before the market crashed.[40]

Trump's first instinct, true to his nature, was dismissal, deflection, and deception. Dismissal began as early as January 22 when he stated, "We have it totally under control," and two days later, "It will all work out well." By February 26 he said, "this is a flu," which of course, it was not. By March 9 he was comparing the twenty-two deaths caused by the virus to the 27,000 to 70,000 each year who die from the common flu, tweeting that with the flu, "nothing is shut down, life & the economy go on." The number of flu deaths in 1990 totaled 100,000, according to his March 4 pronouncements. In reality, the Centers for Disease Control (CDC) reported only 26,582 lives lost during the 1989–90 flu season.[41] Deflection also began early, when Trump blamed immigrants on February 28: "The Democrat policy of open borders is a direct threat to the health and well-being of all Americans. Now you see it with the coronavirus, you see it." He also blamed the press and Democrats: "The Fake News Media and their partner, the Democratic Party, is doing everything within its semi-considerable power (it used to be greater!) to inflame the coronavirus situation, far beyond what the facts would warrant, Surgeon General, 'The risk is low to the average American.'"[42] He blamed Obama for impeding testing for the coronavirus, which "turned out to be very detrimental to what we're doing," even though no Obama-era rule or decision on limiting virus-testing exists. He further argued that Obama ignored the H1N1 (swine flu) epidemic of 2009—which Obama did not, for he immediately declared it a public health emergency.

And finally, the deadliest deception provided false information that could have cost lives. Probably the first deception occurred on February 19 when he argued that by April, during warmer weather, the virus would simply disappear—by early April the death count had surpassed fourteen thousand. Seven days later his administration was stating the virus was contained, arguing US coronavirus numbers "are lower than just about anybody"—they were not. He even took a victory lap, saying that within "a couple of days [it] is going to be down to zero." Nope. By the beginning of March he was stating that Apple was back to full operation in China—it was not; that the pandemic could improve US jobs numbers—it did not; that a vaccine would soon be released—there could be no quick vaccine because clinical trials generally take twelve to eighteen months; and that there were no test shortages, "anyone that wants a test can get a test" to be paid by their insurance company, and some thirty-six hundred had already been tested for the virus—they were not.[43]

As I write these words in mid-2020, the global pandemic crisis continues to unfold. What we know at this point, based on Trump's statements and responses, is that he was more concerned with the health of corporations than the health of the least of these. Echoing the moral reasoning of white Christianity, capitalism is America's religion and its God is the almighty dollar bill. Early during the COVID-19 pandemic, in late March 2020, a suggestion emerged from the so-called prolife community. They called on the elderly to "sacrifice" themselves for the good of the economy. Let our grandparents (those at greater risk of contracting the disease) return to the marketplace and sacrifice their lives to keep the wheels of the economy churning.[44] The often-heard counterargument to Black Lives Matter, that All Lives Matter, has now been proven false. Before our God of capital, it appears that No Lives Matter. Or rather, the lives of corporations are worth more than the lives of our nation's people. As our nation's leaders and the über-rich flee to the safety and seclusion of their mansions, the poor and the elderly are lifted up as a living sacrifice so that the wealthy may have life and have it abundantly.

Obviously, the main reason to minimize an economic recession (or depression) is the negative impact that the party in control might feel on Election Day 2020. The actions of the president and his party were influenced by these political considerations. Regardless of whether a resolution to the pandemic could be achieved in weeks or years, enough has occurred to repudiate any delusions that Trump has supernatural powers or that the United States is protected by God thanks to Trump. The alarm of the coming pandemic was sounded, but the warning was ignored. It wasn't until March 17 that Trump began enlisting the full resources of the federal government to deal with the crisis, as he clearly stated that day, "We are starting the process."[45] Yes, finally! But two months too late! Nevertheless, Trump self-congratulated himself on March 10, noting "had we not acted quickly, the number would have been substantially more."[46] Yes, if only his administration would have acted more quickly, the US would not have been the nation with the most cases in the world starting in early April. What if the administration had persuaded or demanded (through the Defense Production Act) the rapid production of N95 masks and ventilators in February when the warning had originally sounded? What if mask wearing were made mandatory by everyone, including the president? Perhaps countless lives could have been saved during April. What if, instead of focusing on stock values, the administration had focused on human value and the public had been warned earlier to begin practicing social distancing to save lives? What if the administration had forcefully repudiated the misinformation spread by right-wing commentators, whose older audiences were most susceptible to the disease? Would more have begun to self-quarantine earlier and could more lives have been saved? What if the White House's National Security Council Directorate for Global Health Security and Biodefense had not been disbanded in 2017? What if there had been a clear White House–led structure to oversee an early response, when speed is essential to save lives?

And as to that mortal head wound that dispensationalists are expecting? Perhaps it has already occurred as a nonsupernatural response to a natural virus. Maybe the so-called prophecy is a reference to Trump's multiple declarations that he is a stable genius—how else might one explain such an utterance—which might best indicate a severe brain wound?

◆ *One who will be accompanied by a "false prophet" [who] is going to be a devilish John the Baptist*

According to Revelation 13:11–18, a false prophet will arise.[47]
The prophet's job will be to aid and glorify the antichrist
and lead others to swear allegiance. For Hal Lindsey, this
false prophet is—not surprisingly—Jewish. Anti-Semitism,
from viewing Jews as the "killers of Christ" to the future
false prophet who will herald the antichrist of white tribulationists' imagination, provides easy scapegoats. Anti-
Semitic prophets have for millennia unleashed holy fury in
the form of crusades, pogroms, and concentration camps.
The LaHaye and Jenkins duo, in the eighth book of their
Left Behind series titled *The Mark*, introduce as the false
prophet the fictional character Leonardo Fortunato, an Ital-
ian cultural Catholic. The authors tap into anti-Catholic
sentiments held by many Protestants. But the truth of the
matter is that if there are going to be any false prophets, they
have historically been just as numerous among Protestants
as among Jews or Catholics.

Just as there is not just one antichrist, there is also not
just one false prophet. Every generation must deal with
its own false prophets who arise to lead the faithful astray
from the teachings of Jesus. It seems as if today there is a
legion—real people who are not fictional or mythical charac-
ters—ready to forsake God for Trump. When the prosperity
gospel Pentecostal pastor Paula White, with a net worth of
around $5 million, was named to lead the White House's
faith outreach office, she quickly capitalized on her White

House position to fleece sheep. Claiming the power and need to make a holy investment, she appealed to her followers in 2018 to "send me your January paycheck and God will pay you back with interest."[48]

Hypocrisy runs rampant among false prophets. Take for example the Miami Hostel, a gay-friendly youth hostel with an on-site liquor store bought by Jerry Falwell Jr. and his wife Becki in 2013. The chancellor of one of the nation's largest Christian colleges—Liberty University—upon which Junior's father built a religious empire by bashing the queer community (among other things) sees no contradiction in profiting from the gay community. This hypocrisy came to light along with a bizarre friendship between the good reverend, his wife, and a young pool boy they met at the Miami Beach Fontainebleau hotel. This relationship resulted in a $1.8 million promise to the pool boy—who had no business experience—to set up a venture in Miami. The relationship also produced sexually compromising photographs, which allegedly could have been used to blackmail the Falwells. According to Michael Cohen, Trump's former fixer now convicted and serving a prison term, he intervened to obtain and destroy the photos.[49] This intervention might help explain why Falwell, who was on the verge of endorsing Ted Cruz prior to the 2016 Iowa caucus when Cruz was running neck and neck with Trump, instead reneged on his pledge and became the first major evangelical leader to endorse

Trump.[50] The problem here is not owning a gay hostel or with whom consenting adults choose to engage sexually, or the consumption and sale of alcohol. The hypocrisy is in making a fortune through demonizing a group of people while engaging in those very same actions. According to the Liberty University student handbook, the school condemns "homosexual conduct or the encouragement or advocacy of any form of sexual behavior that would undermine the Christian identity or faith mission of the University."[51]

Another example of this hypocrisy can be found in Franklin Graham's righteous indignation over two Latinas' performances during the Super Bowl LV half-time show. Our sense of "moral decency on prime television in order to protect children," according to the reverend, is "disappearing before our eyes."[52] He bemoaned the "sexual exploitation" of women while having nonetheless supported the "grab them by their pussies" president. It is curious that Graham was so troubled by Jennifer Lopez's and Shakira's backsides but not by the multiple naked photos of the First Lady in her previous career as a model, which any Google search can locate. And again, this is not an attempt to body shame women for what they choose to wear or not wear during a photo shoot. This is an attempt to shame men who express moral outrage over women's bodies only when it politically suits them.

It is ironic that, in another example of hypocrisy, Graham pointed to former vice president Joe Biden's son Hunter

Biden in an effort to deflect and detract from questions concerning Trump's shake-down call to the Ukrainian president. "For him to be using his father, while his father was vice president of the United States, to gain monetary value for himself, that should be looked into."[53] Really, someone should introduce Graham to Ivanka, Don, and Erick, who have monetarized the White House in ways unseen since the Gilded Age. Jared Kushner, Trump's son-in-law, took advantage of a special federal program created by the Treasury Department in response to a provision in the 2017 tax laws intended to encourage new development in low-income neighborhoods, so-called opportunity zones. Kushner's start-up company, Cadre, sought to profit from the special tax break included in the law Trump enacted. Although opportunity zones were created to lift poor neighborhoods out of poverty, Cadre targeted neighborhoods in cities already expected to grow wealthier and larger because they provided a more robust return on their investment. In 2017, Kushner's shares in Cadre were listed in his financial disclosure as being worth between $5 to $25 million. His most recent 2020 disclosure lists the value between $25 and $50 million. He will be able to sell his stock in the company, due to a certificate of divestiture from the Office of Government Ethics, without having to pay any capital gains tax due to employment in the federal government. And yet, Graham would have us remain focused on Hunter Biden, whose board membership on Burisma Holdings led to an affiliation with the Ukraine scandal. Let's also not ignore that the only probable reason Franklin even has a platform, or even has a national voice, is due solely to nepotism, capitalizing on his last name.

No doubt Christian evangelicals and Trump make strange bedfellows. The ones who have proclaimed family values for decades have hitched their wagons to an adulterating, thrice-married, porn starlet–paying, sexual-harassing, rape-accused president who also oversees a scandal-ridden administration. Only false prophets could equate Trump, or any politician, or any human, for that matter, with the purity of a holy God. Antichrists from every generation will have their false prophets proclaiming the way, leading many on the wide and easy road leading to perdition. Whenever White, Falwell, Graham, Roberts, Reed, or any other self-proclaimed mouthpiece for God speaks, heralding Trump as touched by God, hold on tightly to your soul and your wallet, for you are in danger of losing both.

The Whore of Babylon

Hal Lindsey probably says it best: "Th[e] Church professes an allegiance to God, but worships a false religious system."[54] The book of Revelation introduces the reader to the "whore of Babylon," a woman, "drunk with the blood of God's holy people" (Rev. 17:1–6).[55] Of course, the word *whore* reveals the sexist bias of historical Christianity, which represents idolatry through the sexuality of a female body. Even though the meaning of the term in this case is not carnal infidelity but religious unfaithfulness, the word reinforces the perceived problem with women's bodies that for centuries has justified Christian misogyny. For Lindsey, the whore is the World Council of Churches.[56] For many other dispensationalists, the whore has been the Roman Catholic Church. In this latter case, the whore was often deemed to be the pope whoring after false doctrines, an interpretation advanced by medieval Catholic reformers and later adopted by Protestants such as Luther, Calvin, and Wesley. Within the Protestant church, the term has come to reinforce anti-Catholic sentiments.

As problematic as the term *whore* has been, it has nonetheless provided a critique of any church throughout history—regardless of denomination or tradition—that is taken by whichever political animal is willing to pay the price of her pimp. The white church, responsible for propping up the antichrist of our day, has played this role, pimped by false prophets for the price of a Supreme Court justice seat and access to the halls of power. Once again, as has always happened throughout Christian history, false prophets proclaimed a man (almost always a man) as the chosen one. When those claiming to be Christians engage in messianic praises of Trump, they demonstrate more of an affinity with cults than with democracies.

The medieval days of popes crowning emperors is long past. Because the United States is not a theocracy, religion can never be the driving force in making political decisions. Yes, our morals and ethics are important for a healthy democracy, whether influenced by our faith, our humanity, or our atheistic philosophical convictions. Damning to democracy is the imposition of doctrines, any doctrines, upon all citizens of a pluralist society. To be crystal clear: no human being, either president or emperor, royalty or prime minister, is God-ordained, because they all fall short of the glory of God. Likewise, no political party, ideology, or social movement—either from the right or from the left—is God-led. Sadly, they are all led by self-interested humans regardless of the lofty rhetoric they expound.

The Last Days

If I had drunk the dispensationalists' Kool-Aid, I guess I would be batshit-scared of the rise of Donald Trump, because no one in our time has better fit the description of the antichrist than he. Fortunately, Donald Trump is not the apocalyptic antichrist prophesied in the biblical text who will bring forth the end of the late great planet earth, because such a figure is simply a fictional figment of the white conservative Christian imagination. He is one of many who have arisen throughout history to lead astray those seeking the face of God. The Trump era will eventually come to an end. If the emboldened racist ethos is not debunked by 46, other antichrists will surely arise in the land. Nevertheless, Trump embodies what white fundamentalist and evangelical Christians have warned us about for generations. And yet, once he appeared, they could not see him as he really is, instead rushing to proclaim him as God's chosen—just as Lindsey and Jenkins predicted. These Christians did not recognize him for what he is because the seduction of political and financial power proved far more desirable than fidelity to even their own skewed interpretation of apocalyptic biblical literature.

To Hell with the Jews

Evangelical Christians, who are major, unwavering supporters of the political state of Israel and consider themselves true friends of the Jews, envision a future for Jews where they burn in hell for all eternity. These friends of Israel have no qualms over the holocaust yet to come. Robert Jeffress, pastor of First Baptist Church of Dallas, one of Trump's twenty-five-member Evangelical Executive Advisory Board, and who led the prayer at the opening of the US embassy in Jerusalem, believes Jews are going to hell.

"Not only do religions like Mormonism, Islam, Judaism, Hinduism, not only do they lead people away from the true God," he preached in a 2009 sermon, "they lead people to an eternity of separation from God in hell."[57] John C. Hagee, a televangelist and leader of a San Antonio megachurch who founded Christians United for Israel makes the shocking claim that Hitler was part of God's plan because he inadvertently returned Jews to Israel.[58] Hitler was part of God's plan?!? Jews simply do not fare well with either the antichrist or their white nationalist Christian friends. According to the Left Behind series, not only are the Jews persecuted by the antichrist during the years of tribulation because of their faith, but they also, upon the final victory of the Christ, are thrown into the lake of fire to burn for all eternity because they rejected the Messiah.

Euro-American Christians' unquestionable commitment to Israel is at the very least disingenuous. Nourished on a steady diet of dispensationalist thought, white conservative Christians believe the second coming of Christ cannot occur until the Second Temple is rebuilt in Jerusalem.[59] Support for Israel has nothing to do with solidarity with a people persecuted throughout history, and who continue to face anti-Semitism today. The support is for purely tactical, apocalyptic reasons. Can white conservative Christians and Jews truly be allies when Christians' cosmology concludes with the annihilation of all Jews, succeeding in the Final Solution where Hitler failed? The state of Israel refuses to hold nationalist Christians accountable for their anti-Semitism because of political expediency. Both Euro-American Christians and the state of Israel are guilty of simply using each other for political gain.

There is no debate regarding the global rise of anti-Semitism, especially among Eurocentric Christians. An obscured aspect of the white nationalist protest in Charlottesville—the one about which President Trump said there are good people on both sides—is what the side wearing white polo shirts and carrying tiki torches chanted: "Jews will not replace us." The anti-Semitism of the Right is overlooked. And yet, the one who dares to criticize the state of Israel runs the risk of being labeled anti-Semitic. The discourse lacks analytical sophistication, for it does not tolerate criticism of a government like Israel's for its abusive practices of occupying Palestinian land. Fear of accusations of anti-Semitism prevents these Christians from distinguishing between the actions of a foreign government and any biases toward its people. The true threat to Israel is not those who push the nation to act more justly toward Palestinians, but their right-wing Christian so-called allies who only see the nation as a means to an end—specifically the end of planet earth. Even though they fantasize about the global final solution to Jewry, a holocaust led by Jesus the warrior in the book of Revelation, their support for Israel, regardless of the oppressive tactics that state uses, is based solely on the role the state plays by ushering in a second coming of Christ, who will bring about their ultimate demise. Israel is sleeping with the enemy, and the most pro-Israel Christians are their deadliest bedfellows.

Christians can never forget their complicity with a faith based on two thousand years of anti-Semitism. We who are Christians must continue to recognize the suffering of our Jewish siblings at our hands. Yet as we stand in solidarity with the targets of anti-Semitism, we cannot look away when a secular state created in their name participates in its own form of oppression, due mainly to the settler colonial policies dating to the Zionist movement of the nineteenth century. The widely cited Zionist slogan "A land without a people for a people without land" ignores the Palestinian inhabitants, in the same way Europeans, ignoring Indigenous people in the Western hemisphere, set out to tame virgin land. Colonialists always see the land as if it had been absent of people. Indians back then and Palestinians today are simply invisible, and if seen, they then stand in the way of the conqueror's manifest destiny. Prime Minister Netanyahu backs this tradition, as demonstrated by his apartheid mentality, which supports settlements on designated Palestinian lands and implements Jim and Jane Crow–type rules to suppress the Palestinian vote. And while lifting up those who are abused does not automatically mean full support of the Palestinians, for some of their political leaders have also engaged in problematic practices, it is nevertheless the Palestinians who are among the least of these due to the consequences of the *nakba*—the enforced evacuations of the Palestinians.

A badass Christianity demands that we stand in solidarity with Palestinians with the same passion by which we must stand with Jews against anti-Semitism. To argue that critiquing a secular state for its failure to establish justice-based policies is anti-Semitic while ignoring Euro-American Christians' fantasies of a final solution is yet another example of gaslighting on the global stage. Anyone who condemns Jews to the fiery pits of hell, who supports Israel only because it ushers their ultimate destruction through Christ's second coming, is an anti-Semite, as are the Israeli politicians who support them for political expedience.

Living in the Shadow of Genocide

No, we cannot all just get along with modern-day antichrists. Nor can we be seduced into thinking that this current antichrist is a historical aberration, a proposition that is advanced by white liberals and moderates. Those appalled by Trump's election, like their conservative skinfolk, continue to hold the delusion that the United States is a Christian nation. Nationalist Christianity refuses to recognize that we live in a society created in the shadow of genocide. Many good-meaning whites numbly asked after Trump's electoral college victory, "How could this have happened?" or intoned, "This is not who we are as a nation." But I argue that this is *exactly* who we are as a nation. Trump does indeed exemplify the United States. In fact, he is the *best example* of what the United States has come to represent. MAGA and WWJD have always been synonymous, long before Trump ever rode down that escalator. Home-grown white supremacy sprouted from the fertile soil of the United States, and its concomitant acts of genocide were made possible through the mainstream, everyday, down-home, good-old-fashioned Christianity of this nation. This white Christianity philosophically and theologically established the inferiority of those who fall short of whiteness so that they could be replaced by those with a delusional sense of exceptionalism. Today's antichrist is simply the culmination of a US white ethnonationalist rhetoric—a rhetoric that permits the US to self-define as the exemplary nation charged with being the shining light unto a darkened world.

Trump's blood-drenched hands are the continuous phantasmagoric legacy of white supremacy and its complicitly silent Christianity. But as horrific as the Trump presidency has been for those on the underside of US white ethnonationalism, this country has endured far worse mass-murdering presidents. Take, for example, the slave-trader and Indian-killer Andrew Jackson, initiator of the Trail of Tears and responsible for the genocidal policies toward the Creek, Seminole, Choctaw, Cherokee, and Chickasaw. "But this is ancient history," whites tell themselves. Many liberals believed modern-day presidents, regardless of partisan politics, still represented the best of American ideals—until Trump. As inhumane as Trump may be, he pales in comparison to other polished presidents of our time whose genocidal policies dwarf the body count even of past presidents like Andrew Jackson.

Probably the modern president with the most blood on his hands, more so than Jackson the Indian-killer, was Richard Nixon—the Quaker. His thirteen secret genocidal operations in Cambodia are responsible for 100,000 Asian deaths and the rise of the Khmer Rouge, a regime so horrific that it is guilty of the genocide of approximately 1.9 million of its own people. Add to this number the 2,279 deaths (not including the 27,255 tortures) caused by Nixon's order to assist in the CIA overthrow of the democratically elected Chilean government in 1973, along with his support—again through the CIA—for Operation Condor, responsible for some 60,000 deaths to support the military dictatorships of not only Chile, but also Argentina, Brazil, Bolivia, Paraguay, and Uruguay. These murderous horrors do not even consider the additional US lives sacrificed to prolong the colonial war in Vietnam or the 81,740 Viet Cong "neutralized" by the CIA

Phoenix Program. Added to the deaths in Southeast Asia is the unknown number of deaths (including US soldiers) resulting from Nixon's decision to use the biological weapon Agent Orange. No other president has more blood on his hands, although Ronald Reagan comes close.

Reagan's collaboration with Central American governments, providing military and financial support to sponsor death squads, led to genocides in Guatemala (about 75,000 mainly Mayan who died during his regime, which can be added to the 200,000 dead in a 1954 CIA-led coup of a democratically elected government), El Salvador (about 75,000 dead), and Honduras (explicit support for the Battalion 316 death squad), not to mention his proxy Contra War in Nicaragua. The reason we have an immigration crisis today can be directly traced to Reagan's genocidal foreign policies in Central America. But the bloodletting was not limited to Central America. Reagan also provided biological weapons to Saddam Hussein, a dictator who had no qualms in using them during the Iran-Iraq war, resulting in approximately 100,000 deaths (per CIA estimates) from US-produced chemical gas.

This list of genocidal presidents must include Bill Clinton. Although Nixon's and Reagan's body counts are larger than those of Jackson, Clinton's numbers are lower. Yes, his hands have less blood on them, but they are no less stained. From the blind eye he cast during the Rwandan genocide, which could have saved 300,000 lives, to his late intervention in the Bosnian atrocities, to his ineptitude in Somalia, hundreds of thousands needlessly perished. To the list we can add Gerald Ford's silence in East Timor and his continuation of Nixon's Operation Condor, George H. W. Bush's economic sanctions against Iraq, which directly led to the death of 1.7 million Iraqis of whom 750,000 were children, or his son George W. Bush's unjustified war there, which caused the death of 1.4 million Iraqis and approximately 4,500 US casualties. So, as bad as Trump may be as president, and as deadly as his policies are toward Latinx people in particular, he still falls short of the satanic, death-causing policies of his most recent imperial predecessors. He did not *create* political hostility toward communities of color; he merely rode out the historical trends to their ultimate conclusion. White fear, whether rooted in Nixon's Southern strategy, or Reagan's outing of mythical welfare queens, or Bush turning murderer Willie Horton into Democrat Michael Dukakis's running mate, is a continued theme that is kept firmly alive through Trump's fearmongering about caravans of immigrants heading our way.

We can see that as bad as Trump might be for Latinx people, the national phobia of Brown bodies did not begin with Trump, nor did his anti-immigrant policies appeared *ex nihilio*. The moderate Democrat Bill Clinton is responsible for the implementation of the border policy of deterrence. Passage of the North American Free Trade Agreement (NAFTA) meant the United States would soon face an explosion of immigrants crossing the southern border. Within months of ratifying NAFTA, Operation Gatekeeper, based on a policy of "prevention through deterrence," was established. The rationale for a prevention strategy, according to an August 2001 letter by Richard M. Stana of the US General Accounting Office, was "to make it so difficult and costly for aliens to attempt illegal entry that fewer individuals would try."[60] "Costly" was doublespeak for loss of life. Pushed by the militarization of former points of entry, migrants would die traversing dangerous terrain and hazardous lands. Their deaths—as collateral damage—would be viewed by Americans as an acceptable cost because it would serve to *deter* others from undertaking the perilous crossing. Clinton allowed the horrific death of migrants as an integral component of the "prevention through deterrence" policy. After years of gathering empirical data, we can conclude no one was deterred. Instead, there were more deaths on the border.

Clinton's successor, George W. Bush, who ran on the promise of compassionate conservatism and was beloved by many as a friend to the Latinx community, demonstrated a total lack of compassion by orchestrating the largest Immigration and Customs Enforcement (ICE) raid in US history. On May 12, 2008, the Agriprocessor slaughterhouse and meat packing plant at Postville, Iowa, was raided by some 900 agents from the FBI, ICE, state troopers, and a variety of government agencies. Race and ethnicity determined who was detained. Trump's immediate predecessor, Barack Obama, the first Black president, earned the moniker "Deporter-in-Chief" for expatriating more Brown bodies than all previous presidents combined. Worse, he ordered the construction of for-profit prisons to house these families, placing Brown children, whose only crime was being born on the wrong side of the border, behind bars.

Genocidal presidential oppressors are not listed here to exonerate Trump, even though his ineptitude is most likely responsible for making his murderous policies less effective or efficient than those of his predecessors. The piled-up slew of nonwhites' corpses is provided here to demonstrate how those who were chosen to lead the empire were elected by those who have been the majority group, the white people who see themselves as God-loving and God-fearing Christians. But if they were truly Christians, we would have to question this white God who was deaf during these recent genocides, just as the God who was silent while his so-called chosen people, heirs of a new Jerusalem, were engaged in the genocide of their neighbors. This white God may have made "his" home in white churches who justify genocide, but this deity is actually the angel of darkness masquerading as an angel of light. All gods who are unable to speak in the face of great oppression, or who twist us into believing that this oppression is somehow justified, must be killed, whether they be the God of *pax americana*, the God of militarism, the God of nationalism, the God of Republicans, or the God of Democrats. All gods who privilege a chosen people because of their race, class, gender, religious affiliation, or sexual orientation and condemn others to death must likewise die, and we no longer can patiently wait for God's demise. We must hasten this God's death. Our very survival requires us to dig the graves for this American nationalist Christianity as quickly as possible.

Eurocentric nationalist Christianity is the problem, the primary reason for the division, discord, and dissension prevalent throughout the United States. Unless we commit to burying once and for all this malignant manifestation of the white gospel, it will be the cause of this nation's demise. The nation simply cannot move forward if this white supremacist ideology continues to play an overblown role in the lives of so many. White Christianity must be totally and utterly rejected and amputated from the nation-body. I want to be clear in saying that rejection of the nationalist Christianity of whites should not be confused with rejection of Christianity. What must be rejected are the Eurocentric lenses by which Christianity is seen and defined. A badass Christianity has the audacity to see through the lens of the disenfranchised, the marginalized, the oppressed—to define through their own cultural symbols. Rejecting white Christianity for one that disinherited communities can embrace means that the dominant nationalist Christianity is simply beyond reform.

The type of reform white Christianity sought during the twentieth century simply became a means of better masking the horror of its immovable white supremacy. The liberal or progressive solutions offered were mere cosmetic tinkering with the racist status quo. Think of the Social Gospel of the early twentieth century, rooted in an idea of Manifest Destiny that celebrated the conquest of lands and civilizations belonging to and occupied by others. Or the Niebuhrian mid-century response that provided religious justification for the establishment of a neoconservatism that advocated the global domination of so-called inferior countries and cultures. Or even the Hauerwasian understanding of a justice that took hold within white Christian churches toward the end of the century that dismissed and demonized those who sought a social ethics that responded to institutionalized racism and ethnic discrimination. These representations of white Christianity have led to a church that called advocacy for justice an error. The Niebuhrian constipation of mid-century simply led to a severe case of Hauerwasian bowel blockage by century's end. But there is good news available for dealing with the prevailing and predominant religious shitstems they created. From the underside of whiteness, liberative balm emerges that can bring relief to the white Christian body full of the manure of supremacism.

5

Badass Prophets

Jonah was a badass prophet. It doesn't matter whether he actually existed or was simply a fictional character designed to teach us moral lessons about God and human nature. The story of Jonah being called to visit his tormentors with an offer of God's clemency and compassion makes for a really good moralistic yarn. Yes, like Pinocchio, Jonah was indeed swallowed by a whale (or at least a big fish). But focusing on the really big fish part of the story and not the prophet's ironic homework assignment only distracts our attention from the story's main message. Imagine today if God were to tell an undocumented Latinx immigrant to go to the Trump White House and preach repentance. Or if God were to give a similar call to an African American to visit the tiki torch–carrying organizers of the Unite the Right rally. Jonah's God demands that the disinherited go to the very thieves who stole their basic human rights and dignity to tell them they should seek out salvation.

Can you blame Jonah for running in the opposite direction of the Assyrians? Or would you fault him, after his halfhearted attempt at preaching God's mercies, for sitting up on a hill overlooking the city, gleefully waiting for God to rain down fire and brimstone upon his oppressors? After all, these are the same oppressors who would ultimately annihilate the northern kingdom of Israel. One can only shake one's head in disbelief at this baffling notion: that Jonah is told by God to save a population who would eventually come and destroy his own people. There seems to be a certain sadism to God's calling in this situation. Who can blame Jonah for being pissed off? Jonah is a badass for demanding justice—a retributive justice—from what appears to be an unjust God. God instead calls for reconciliation. But is reconciliation even possible? Can those who are repressed today by structures of whiteness kiss and embrace those seeking their subjugation?

Can the consequences of oppression ever really be remedied? Can Black bodies in the South or Brown bodies in the Southwest ever arise from their deaths to offer friendship to those who tied nooses around their necks? Can they fellowship with the complicit millions who continue to benefit, to this day, from the unearned power, profit, and privileges purchased through and by lynching? Can Indigenous bodies simply move on (and to where?) as the descendants of settlers, secure in knowing they possess binding title to stolen property, offer insincere apologies? Are whites or God asking too much of communities of color, demanding they be good Uncle Toms or coconuts and just forget how they continue to be treated? Be good Christians and simply get over it? Forgive and forget?

Jonah knew the answer was no. How can the dispossessed become one with those benefiting from their dispossession, while the latter refuse to even recognize a need exists for repentance and desires even less to have fraternity? The dominant culture, despite its reconciling rhetoric, will never seek justice-based praxis because they are fully aware any creation of a more just and perfect union will cost them their unearned station within society. To embrace in fraternity while continuing to secure and support oppressive social structures has always proven deadly from the time of Jonah to our present age. And here is why progress in seeking a more just union is so damn hopeless. We have no historical example of those who benefit from oppressive structures—whether it be Assyrians back then or the Euro-Americans today—renouncing their unearned power, profit, and privilege for the sake of creating a more just society. Sadly, any advances, no matter how minor, have always been accompanied by the blood of the dispossessed flowing in the streets.

Jonah's badass resistance to God's call to reconcile with

his enemies raises a crucial question for our time: reconcile to what, exactly? Reconciliation connotes seeking concurrence in incongruencies (as in reconciling one's checkbook) or in relationships (as in seeking reconciliation through a marriage counselor). It's an attempt to restore harmony to a once-amicable relationship that now finds itself in conflict, while the need to resolve the conflict becomes the driving force behind endeavors to reconcile. But how can restoration occur if the interests of nationalist Christianity's devotees were, from the beginning, never "of one accord" with the communities of color yearning to breathe free? There is nothing to restore because there was never unanimity to begin with. Seeking reconciliation, therefore, is a lost cause. We must demand, instead, the creation of a new way of being, a new way of relating to each other, a new way of governing ourselves. Jonah may have been a badass, but he failed to connect any repentance, any forgiveness, or any salvation with a demand for justice in order to create a new way of relating. Maybe if the demand for justice had been a component of the call to Assyria to repent, then the northern kingdom of Israel would not have fallen in 772 BCE and the ten lost tribes would not have disappeared from history.

If white Christians claim to follow Jesus, it only makes sense that they follow what he claimed is the greatest commandment, upon which all the laws and prophets are based: "You shall love the Lord your God with all your heart, and with all your soul, and with all your mind, [and] you shall love your neighbor as yourself" (Matt. 22:37–40 NRSV). Love for both God and neighbor become an outward expression of an inward conversion. If a tree is indeed known by its fruit, then the absence of love for neighbors of color, queer neighbors, non-Christian neighbors, and immigrant neighbors demonstrates very clearly that nationalist Christianity will always fail to repent, seek forgiveness, and obtain salvation. Salvation and liberation can never be achieved if love for God and neighbor are nonexistent. We should not rush to find harmony with our God and our neighbor without dealing with the sorrow and hopelessness of Holy Saturday. We must avoid the temptation to seek a premature peace because, as it did for the Northern Kingdom, it would lead to the obliteration of communities of color. The act of reconciliation, the opportunity for salvation, and the hope of liberation are cheapened when justice is sacrificed for the sake of serenity for the dominant culture. Nationalist Christianity's continued refusal to dismantle the very structures built to uphold their unjustified power, profits, and privilege signifies a preference for accruing the unmerited dividends of supremacism. Justice is not a bargaining chip used in negotiating among political adversaries. Justice leads to spiritual healing. The phrase often repeated at protest rallies—"No Justice, No Peace"—still rings true.

Yes, the marginalized should seek reconciliation with

their God and neighbor, a reconciliation rooted in justice. Ignoring this call dismisses the good news preached by Jesus. Regrettably, the salvation preached from pulpits in white Christian churches all too often ignores white Christians' complicity with the social and political structures responsible for so much of the social division over race, ethnicity, gender, class, and sexual orientation. These sermons become empty words lacking any significance. For white Christians, the gospel mirrors the values of the dominant culture, advocating a Christianity that nauseates the saints. A clarion call for a badass Christianity rooted in the rejection of nationalist Christianity could prevent marginalized communities from devolving into the race war that appears to be so coveted by those losing their white affirmative action.

The South Will Rise Again

The politically correct, kinder, and gentler manifestation of racism in the form of color-blind advocacy may have been an effective tool during the last quarter of the last century, but with the election of a Black man to the highest office, white Christians saw that a more radical strategy was required or else white America would be lost forever. The old battle cry that "the South will rise again" moved from the geographically specific to a national ethos. For over a century and a half, a portion of America believed that a superior way of life, a more gentlemanly Southern civilization, had been vanquished through unjustified Northern aggression. A romanticization of an elegant and genteel antebellum Southern culture took hold of the American conscious. And although the Southern cause was lost, this glamorized bygone era morphed into and thrived as Jim and Jane Crow.

Probably no group is more responsible for preserving and glorifying Southern racism than white women. In 1894 the United Daughters of the Confederacy (UDC) was founded to rehabilitate Confederate history by portraying its soldiers and leaders as heroic figures sacrificing their lives for a lost cause. The UDC spearheaded the effort to erect monuments and statues to these heroes throughout the South. The symbols of what they saw as a superior culture built on slavery were revived by these white women, and this culture remains alive in the hearts of many who continue, to this day, to cling to the symbols signifying that way of thinking and being. Proudly waving Confederate flags, preserving statues of generals of the defeated army, reframing the cause of the war from the defense of slavery and white supremacy to states' rights, members of the UDC attest to the underlying desire for the South to one day rise again, like a phoenix from the ashes of our nation's Civil War.

Even President Trump expressed nostalgia for those golden days when, shortly after the violent 2017 white nationalist rally in Charlottesville, he said, "Sad to see history and culture of our great nation being ripped apart with the removal of our beautiful statues and monuments."[1] The hope of racists, rekindled by words like those, is that the lost cause will one day be found so that a new nation—not just the South but the entire Union—can be born again. This South will no longer be located in just our southern states, because the South is very much alive and well in the North, the West, the Midwest, and the Southwest. Today, this white supremacist do-over seeks an opportunity to overturn the 1865 conclusion of that terrible war. The urgency for such a do-over has little to do with whites pining for the good old days of the early eighteenth century but more to do with their lament over the present-day loss of white affirmative action.

In the ultimate gaslighting move, whites, suffering from a victimhood complex, have been spinning a false narrative of persecution. Feeling ignored and forgotten by their government, which instead seems to be privileging undeserving minority groups, they justify their anger and resentment and further fuel their fear of slipping into minority status within what was once a nation created exclusively for whiteness. Whites in their demographic downward cycle fight back for what they believe has been taken from them: their birthright to white affirmative action. The final jolt electrifying national white supremacist resolve was the election of a Black man to the White House in 2008, a historic event activating the quick mobilization of resistance groups such as the Tea Party movement. President Obama's dark skin pigmentation became an immediate issue that proved his lack of worthiness to hold office, along with Trump's demand to see Obama's birth certificate (which, when produced, was dismissed as fake) and rumors circulating that Obama was Muslim (which he is not—not that it should matter). When white supremacists pronounced Obama's middle name, Hussein, they gave the clear message that Muslims cannot be considered Americans, as well as offering implied or overt racial slurs. The Obama presidency was, in the minds of white nationalist supremacists, a bizarre fluke that would henceforth be corrected in 2012 when the White House would be made white again. However, Obama's second term launched the mainstreaming of an escalated white nationalist supremacist hysteria: the beginning of the "American carnage" to which Trump alluded during his inaugural speech. In 2012, Bill O'Reilly of Fox News captured the ensuing white rout on election night, lamenting, "The white establishment is now the minority. And the voters, many of them, feel that the economic system is stacked against them and they want stuff . . . the demographics are changing, it's not a traditional America anymore."[2]

Trump was the savior whites had been waiting for since that fateful 2012 election night, an antichrist who would scrub away the blackness they feared had infected the White House. Whites suffering from fragility exchanged their votes for promises of reclaiming the lost America that O'Reilly had lamented four years earlier, where those who had been relegated to the margins must once again know their correct place, taught through centuries of white terrorism. Trump's campaign slogan, Make America Great Again—shorthand for restoring, strengthening, and expanding white affirmative action—is best demonstrated by the intentional, deliberate, and carefully orchestrated reversal of practically all of Obama's policies, initiatives, and laws—a literal attempt to erase him.

But winning at the voting booth is not enough. Changing demographics are rapidly relegating whites to minority status. Democratic principles would undo centuries of racist majority rule, policies, and legislation. Fearing the demands made by communities of color to share in the fruits of the Republic, whites reinterpreted such demands as a mandate to replace them and as a threat to white unearned profit, power, and privilege. White nationalist supremacists maintain that what is needed to restore the balance of power in their favor is to usher in the race war they have been expecting ever since the minor gains made by communities of color during the Civil Rights movements. Despite the best intentions of communities of color to seek a new, just, and reconciled social order, nationalist Christianity remains bent on bringing about a race war. Their fantasy is that such a race war would rescue white ethnonationalist Christianity. Well-meaning whites continue to ignore their own history of massacring people of color, specifically Indians since the founding of the Republic and Blacks since the close of the Civil War. Their white church-going ancestral failure to fully domesticate the Blacks in their communities led to the carnage at Rosewood, Florida; the burning of Black Wall Street in Tulsa, Oklahoma; the bloodbath of Milan, Georgia; and the killing fields of Elaine, Arkansas—to name but a few of these horrific bouts of ethnic and racial cleansing. White Christian terrorism was not limited to mass killings, however. The daily lynching of Blacks in the South and Latinx people in the Southwest, at times on Sundays after church picnics, testifies to how normal the killing of nonwhites has always been, while at the same time it is interwoven into the United States religious tapestry.

Racing toward a Race War

With the advances of the Civil Rights movement and the enforcement of anti-lynching laws, whites lost an important disciplinary technology for keeping people of color in line through intimidation. Fearful of retaliation, whites armed themselves with military assault weapons, which they said was their Second Amendment right—in preparation for the coming race war, over which they continue to salivate. The right to bear arms is not just for self-defense, when a pistol would be adequate, or for hunting, when a single or double-barrel shotgun would suffice. Bearing arms has been redefined for offensive purposes. The purpose of semiautomatic firearms, which were invented for the purpose of war, is to kill as many people as possible without reloading. Why else would hundreds of thousands or most likely millions of people across the United States need to accumulate military hardware? As in some popularized zombie horror flick, the goal is to kill as many as possible of the invading horde trying to bring white civilization to its knees. But until that fateful day, if children's brains happen to be blown out while these children sit in classrooms studying history, then they become acceptable collateral damage, sacrifices presented to Moloch, small offerings to the white God as the cost of vigilance for the race war that lies ahead.

Think of the popular 1971 ultimate supremacist novel *The Turner Diaries*, which describes a not-so-distant future when an underground white supremacist army overthrows the US government, which is controlled by Jews who are able to manipulate Blacks without repercussion by dim-witted white liberals. One of the novel's subplots recounts how the guerilla unit of the fictional Earl Turner detonated a homemade bomb of fuel oil and fertilizer concealed in a truck at FBI headquarters at 9:15 a.m. In a frightening example of life imitating art, in 1995 Timothy McVeigh took inspiration from the novel and one day at 9:02 a.m. blew up the Alfred P. Murrah Federal Building in Oklahoma City, which housed an FBI field office. He used a homemade bomb of fuel oil and fertilizer concealed in a truck. Clippings of the novel were mailed to his sister, and a passage from the novel was found in McVeigh's getaway car.[3]

McVeigh was not the only man hoping his terrorist act would ignite a race war. Think of Charles Manson, who tattooed a swastika on his forehead. In 1969 he used racism to manipulate and incite his disciples to kill, with the hope of sparking a race war in which he would triumphantly lead whites to victory over Blacks.[4] Among the many confessions of mass murderers hoping to ignite a race war are those of the 2015 shooter at a Bible study at the Emanuel African Methodist Episcopal Church in Charleston[5] and the more recent 2019 Walmart shooter in El Paso.[6] No doubt more blood will be spilled in hopes of lighting the spark that ignites the racism powder keg. Acts of mass killing for the purpose of detonating a race war, similar to those from *The Turner Diaries*, are increasing with such frequency that the FBI has determined race-based violence is now a national threat with a priority greater than foreign terrorism.[7]

Naive, or perhaps unwilling to admit the truth of the underlying social ethos responsible for these national, race-based violent killings, white Christians erroneously dismiss mass shootings as acts carried out by demented lone wolves. Examining the rhetoric used by President Trump and alt-right pundits such as Tucker Carlson, Ann Coulter, and Rush Limbaugh demonstrates a striking degree of overlap between the words they used to refer to the undocumented and the language used by the murderer of twenty-two people at the El Paso Walmart in his twenty-three-hundred-word post on the 8chan website explaining his motives. He used words like *invasion* and *replacement*, words that had been relegated to the fringes of the nation's alt-right, but since 2018 have become a shared vocabulary mainstreamed by cable television and radio personalities, along with the politicians for whom they advocate.[8]

According to Congressman Max Rose and former FBI special agent Ali H. Soufan, "We both risked our lives to fight al Qaeda. But the enemy we currently face is not a jihadist threat. It's white supremacists—in the United States and overseas." Since 9/11, more Americans were killed on US soil by white supremacists than by jihadist terrorists, and yet white supremacists are not referred to as terrorists. Why? Why has no white supremacist group ever been designated as a terrorist organization under federal law? Congressional hearings reveal that today's supremacists are organizing in a similar fashion to jihadist terrorist groups during the 1980s and '90s. According to FBI director Christopher Wray, US supremacists are traveling overseas (mainly to the battlegrounds of Ukraine) for paramilitary training. More than twice as many whites traveled to Ukraine to join the civil war than those who traveled to Afghanistan—the birthplace of al Qaeda—to fight in their war in the 1980s. Several of those who trained in Ukraine were responsible for fomenting violence in Charlottesville during the Unite the Right rally in 2017. As long as the government refuses to name the activities of white supremacist mass murders as a terrorist acts, the investigative arm of the government cannot provide an adequate response to this clear and present danger to the Republic. [9]

Increases in white supremacist terrorism are so likely that New Jersey's annual Terrorism Threat Assessment of 2020 not only raised the likelihood of a future attack to "high" but also announced that a domestic threat would be more likely to occur than threats from ISIS and al Qaeda combined. From 2018 to 2019, hate group use of propaganda such as flyers, posters, stickers, and handouts increased from 1,215 to 2,713 incidents. According to the report, "Some white supremacist extremists argue that participating in mass attacks or creating other forms of chaos will accelerate the imminent and necessary collapse of society in order to build a racially pure nation."[10] In a disturbing demonstration of updating a past strategy used by whites to clear the land of Indians—by giving them blankets infected with smallpox— today's neo-Nazis and white supremacists are encouraging members who contract COVID-19 to spread the contagion among Jews by coughing on synagogue doorknobs.[11] Known as "accelerationists," these neo-Nazis embrace apocalyptic visions of the crumbling of civilization so that their new thousand-year reign can be created upon the ruins of the old world; COVID-19 is simply their secret weapon.[12]

Not only does the COVID pandemic provide an opportunity to usher in a race war; so too do the 2020 predominantly peaceful protests concerning police brutality toward communities of color. Take for example the "boogaloo bois," a loose coalition of far-right supremacist extremists who are actively seeking a second civil race war that would replace our current political system with a white ethnostate. They are recognizable by the festive floral Hawaiian shirts they wear while clad in armored vests, carrying assault rifles. The term "boogaloo" has become code language for civil war.[13] Originally, they were showing up at state capitals during COVID-19 lockdown resistance. Since the start of protests in the wake of the Floyd murder, they have attended peaceful demonstrations in dozens of major US cities seeking to stir racial conflict.[14] On May 30, 2020, three boogaloo bois (all with US military backgrounds) were arrested heading toward a Black Lives Matter protest in Las Vegas in possession of Molotov cocktails and numerous firearms, hoping to incite violence. In Oakland, California, two others were charged with killing a courthouse guard. Impersonating activists, they seek to infiltrate and co-opt peaceful protests to ignite violence that could create enough confusion that it might generate riots.[15]

They even created a Twitter account—@ANTIFA_US—impersonating a left-leaning group and calling for violence during the protests. At the very least, they hope to frame and blame peaceful protestors for riots and civil unrest that threaten the security of whites in hopes of sparking a civil war. Taking the bait, Trump and his attorney general, William Barr, have blamed peaceful protestors for the escalating violence instigated by these right-wing extreme hate groups.[16]

Should we then be surprised that during the coronavirus lockdowns the Trump administration recommended states categorize gun shops as critical businesses that should remain open?[17] White nationalists may want a race war even though people of color have refused to arm and prepare. Maybe this is a mistake. Or maybe after being the recipients of centuries of violence, communities of color find it difficult to reconcile unconditional love with possessing instruments of hatred that kill. But then again, white nationalist Christianity, since its inception at the start of the colonial venture, has a history of reconciling their gospel with killing, raping, and pillaging.

The ease with which the call for a race war puts on religious garb is frightening. Even today, one of the top terms used to search the internet for supremacist material is "Ra-HoWa"—Racial Holy War.[18] Race war, for white nationalists, is a holy calling in which those who make sacrifices for the cause are referred to as saints.[19] Rather than proclaiming the gospel message of love, nationalist Christian ministers use their public pulpit to lift up fear, mistrust, and anger toward their opponents, pointing to a savior created in their image—an unholy trinity of Trump as the father, Fox pundits as the son, and white supremacy as the holy spirit. And before whites who do not belong to white supremacy hate groups dismiss these claims, reassuring themselves they abhor the idea of a race war, they should realize their commitment to ignore and do nothing—or worse, to vote and support enablers of supremacist attitudes—speaks volumes to their complicity. It makes no difference whether those seeking mass murder are jihadists or white nationalist Christians—terrorism is terrorism is terrorism is terrorism.

Mainstreaming White Nationalist Christian Terrorism

White Christianity soft-pedals the nationalist alt-right radical rhetoric as something tolerable. Such religious reframing of white supremacy is not a new phenomenon, for the practice has been a crucial factor, since the forming of the Republic, to secure ample space for whiteness to flourish. Today's apologists for white nationalist supremacism continue the long tradition of mainstreaming white hatred by presenting the political as the realization of the spiritual. Take, for example, Euro-American Christian leaders such as Trump's spiritual advisor Paula White. During an interview with disgraced televangelist Jim Bakker (who in 2020 started hawking a snake oil that he claimed could cure coronavirus[20]), she agreed that if Trump is not reelected, "we're going to lose the freedom of America soon." For Ms. White, and many whites, the powers of darkness are aligned against Trump. In response, she calls Christians to take a stand. "It's a battle of righteousness [against] wickedness," she said. She is not alone in her views. Religious talk radio host and *New York Times* bestselling author Eric Metaxas and others participate in the ultimate shameless act of gaslighting by comparing opposition to Trump with how the Nazis took over Germany.[21] All these false prophets agree that if Trump fails in his reelection bid, America will come to an end. For them, a spiritual battle is raging, and Christians are being called to fight the darkness of moderates and liberals who are out to destroy America because they are against Trump, ergo, against God.

But others see this spiritual battle as also physical. An assemblage of false prophets calls for physical violence against the enemies of Trump and God. Take, for example, the remarks made during the 2020 impeachment procedures by Robert Jeffress, pastor of First Baptist Dallas, who during a *Fox & Friends* interview said, "I do want to make this prediction . . . if the Democrats are successful in removing the president from office, I'm afraid it would cause a civil war-like fracture in this nation from which this country will never heal."[22] Franklin Graham seems to agree, issuing dire warnings that "our country could begin to unravel if an elected president is thrown out of office because of lies and the media."[23] Unable to defend the president's actions, defenders instill fear of a possible civil war if they do not get their way. And while Jeffress hints at civil war, Rick Wiles, pastor of Flowing Streams Church, founder of the conservative platform *TruNews*, and a conspiracy theorist best known for his warnings against Jewish world domination, portrays immigrants as a "brown invasion" used by God to punish white Americans for legalizing abortion.[24] He predicts a civil war

> if they take [Trump] out. . . . However he leaves there's going to be violence in America. . . . There are people in this country, veterans, there are cowboys, mountain men, I mean guys that know how to fight. And they're going to make a decision that the people that did this to Donald Trump are not going to get away with it and they're going to hunt them down. I'm serious, they're going to hunt them down. . . . If these people in Washington think that they're going to get away with it, it's not going to happen. The Trump supporters are going to hunt them down. It's going to happen and this country is going to be plunged into darkness and they brought it upon themselves because they won't back off.[25]

White Christian nationalists seeking harm for opponents and people of color are not only a crucial component of Trump's base, but they have found a voice within his administration. Political figures within the Republican Party and the Trump administration have increasingly adopted the language and memes of white supremacist hate groups, and through the power of their office, they mainstream those views. For example, the vast majority of Latinx people in this country share a common experience, the vile racist retort of "Go back to where you came from!" It doesn't matter that many have occupied this land for generations and centuries before the latest "illegal" immigrants to this land—whites—ever showed up. The pain of this phrase, heard by generations of Latinx people, is so raw that the US Equal Employment Opportunity Commission lists "Go back to where you came from" as an example of "harassment based on national origin."[26]

Yet, in spite of this painful slur of not belonging, Trump, on July 14, 2019, tweeted,

> So interesting to see "Progressive" Democrat Congress-women, who originally came from countries whose governments are a complete and total catastrophe, the worst, most corrupt and inept anywhere in the world (if they even have a functioning government at all), now loudly and viciously telling the people of the United States, the greatest and most powerful nation

on earth, how our government is to be run. Why don't they go back and help fix the totally broken and crime infested places from which they came. Then come back and show us how it is done. These places need your help badly, you can't leave fast enough. I'm sure that Nancy Pelosi would be very happy to quickly work out free travel arrangements!

His racist tweet was geared toward four first-term US Representatives to Congress, all women of color, namely Representatives Alexandria Ocasio-Cortez of New York, Ilhan Omar of Minnesota, Ayanna Pressley of Massachusetts, and Rashida Tlaib of Michigan. They are all US citizens and all, except Omar, are US-born.

Not surprisingly, white nationalists praise the president whenever he tweets xenophobic comments. One hate group unashamedly tweeted, "This is the Kind of WHITE NATIONALISM we elected him for."[27] When white Christians and government officials adopt the language of white supremacists, they unleash a wave of public racist rhetoric as Trump's devotees demonstrated during political rallies by chanting "Send her back!" in response to his tweet concerning the four congresswomen of color. Fascinating how the phrase "I was an immigrant and you welcomed me" is now totally ignored by the religious right. Most white evangelical Republicans (93 percent) favor restrictive immigration policies.[28] But why should we be surprised when white Christians fail to grasp the deep roots of their faith's racism? The majority of people of color—77 percent of Blacks, 69 percent of Latinx people, and 59 percent of other races or ethnicities—believe Trump encourages white supremacy.[29] A slight majority of white Americans (57 percent) also believe Trump's decisions, behavior, and actions have encouraged white supremacist groups. The majority of those who would disagree is mainly comprised of Republicans (74 percent) and white evangelicals (70 percent). Since that first day Trump came down that escalator, using racially divisive phrases to amplify the anxieties of white Christians has been his signature style during all of his rallies. In the midst of social unrest triggered by the George Floyd murder under the knee of police repression, Trump addressed the nation at Mount Rushmore on July 3, 2020. He described mostly peaceful protests as "violent mayhem" by "angry mobs" unleashing a "wave of violent crime" to "cancel culture." He went on to say, "The radical ideology attacking our country advances under the banner of social justice. But in truth, it would demolish both justice and society. . . . They want to silence us, but we will not be silenced."[30] Stoking white Christian fears, inciting fear of advocates of social justice, and promoting hatred toward others has translated into Trump-affirming votes. Why give up such a winning combination?

Probably no other member of Trump's team is more responsible for mainstreaming anti-Latinx hatred than the senior advisor to the president—Stephen Miller. Miller's e-mails to the alt-right news network Breitbart were leaked, revealing his white nationalist racist conspiracies concerning white genocide being committed by people of color. The architect of Muslim travel bans and Latinx family separation, Miller has regularly promoted theories popular with white supremacist groups. For example, he had no qualms about forwarding racist material from the white nationalist website *VDare*. When nine Black worshipers were shot by a white nationalist in Charleston, his primary concern was about the removal of Confederate paraphernalia from e-commerce websites. In one e-mail defending the Confederate flag he wrote, "Should the cross be removed from immigrant communities, in light of the history of the Spanish conquest?"[31]

Miller's words and policies, like those of other administrators of his ilk, institutionalize violence. From the safety of their government offices, they don't need to worry about the blood of immigrants splattering on their well-polished wingtip shoes. Nevertheless, their hands remain stained in the blood of the alien among us, and these stains refuse to be washed away no matter how vigorously they rinse their hands. The institutionalization of violence by government officials such as Miller is responsible for many personal attacks faced by communities of color, reaching a sixteen-year high in 2018, with a significant upswing in violence directed at Latinx people.[32] There is a link between the anti-Latinx rhetoric and policies employed by Miller and company in the halls of power and the violence committed against Latinx people on the streets of the country.

Latinx groups are not alone in bearing the brunt of hatred generated by the White House. When President Trump wrongly referred to COVID-19 by the racist term "Chinese virus,"[33] he unleashed a wave of Sinophobia. Within days of his insisting on using the term, the Asian American community began to experience discriminatory acts and violence. Many were spit upon or harassed as strangers shouted "f*ck China" on the streets of San Francisco. In New York City, a twenty-three-year-old woman was punched in the face as her female assailant made anti-Asian slurs. During the last week of March 2020 alone, 650 acts of racism, xenophobia, and anti-Asian hate crime were reported throughout the nation.[34] Surely the number of incidents is much higher when we consider that many simply do not report such ethnic-based confrontations—I know I never did.

You know you have a problem with government officials mainstreaming supremacy rhetoric when Twitter employees, who developed an algorithmic solution to report and suspend neo-Nazi and white supremacist accounts, soon expressed concerns with its implementation because a number of Republican politicians would be flagged.[35] Such politicians, along with Miller's race-based obsession with Latinx people, have legitimized the normalcy of putting

Brown children in cages. And yet ironically, the ones that nationalist Christians fear and upon whom they are willing to wage war are, in fact, the Jonahs from whom they can discover forgiveness from God and liberation from their sins of commission and omission. The outcast, the unwanted, the stone rejected by the builder, all become the cornerstone by which whites can find their salvation. Like Jonah, communities of color are called to preach that the modern-day Assyrians, the world's conquerors, should put away their white gods and bow their knees to the God of the oppressed. From the margins arises the opportunity for white Christians to repent from the nationalist Christianity they constructed and through solidarity with those for whom they have denied life find their own life.

Becoming a Badass

The major obstacle to becoming one body in Christ remains the dominant culture's refusal to even believe there is a problem—and they are the problem. A "Karen" can always be found to falsely accuse a Black person, as Amy Cooper did in Central Park. No doubt we, like Jonah, have a righteous craving to sit on the mountaintop and witness God's wrath rain down upon those who hate our nonwhite bodies. But as satisfying as this event might be, a badass Christianity remains rooted in uncompromising agape love, a love that pities those who have been taught since childhood to hate. What does it mean to love white Christian goats? Ignorant of how their faith has been manipulated to privilege their political and economic whiteness, they require pity from badass sheep more than hatred or revenge. But pity does not mean immediate forgiveness, even though it may be offered on an individual basis if it contributes to the healing of the one injured. We must withhold this forgiveness of the dominant culture—as an act of love—until the dominant culture repents and moves toward becoming new creatures committed to establishing justice. Withholding forgiveness from the dominant culture for their centuries of ethnic and racial genocide is an actual attempt, rather than a theoretical or rhetorical one, to move toward becoming one body. Because the prerequisite to liberation is repentance, for the hope of whites' salvation we must withhold forgiveness.

What then do we do as we wait for hardened, stony hearts to crack and split, becoming a contrite broken offering unto the Lord?—because only when the heart is broken can God's grace seep in. As communities of color continue to wait for the day when whites discover their salvation and liberation through them, we must continue our call to stand in solidarity with the least of these. We are called to implement a badass Christianity, badass because it is a radical way of living that can literally turn the world upside-down. In my previous book, *Burying White Privilege*, I offered a brief list to describe this badass Christianity. In this closing chapter, we must not only revisit the list but also add some flesh to the badass skeleton. So—what is a badass Christianity?

Decolonization of a Liberating Faith Expression

> [Badass Christianity is] . . . decolonization of a liberating faith expression intended to upset the prevailing social order designed to maintain neoliberalism.

White liberals love to get arrested. For them, an arrest demonstrates liberal street creds. Every so often, some of my well-meaning white students ask me to join them in some act of civil disobedience for the sake of being incarcerated. "Thank you, but no," I respond. "Occupying a Latinx body means I don't have to try to get arrested. Because of racial profiling, it comes naturally." And while certain situations may call for placing one's body on the line, knowing the end result might be incarceration or worse, as people of color we must do everything we can *not* to join a prison population where the majority of the inhabitants already look like us. Whenever I have been detained, I have worked hard not to be incarcerated, for if I am, this street cred comes at too steep of a price, because funds and resources are spent to keep me out of prison rather than going to advance the cause. How does one engage in radical praxis that disrupts oppressive structures designed to maintain white supremacy without the rashness or foolhardiness that might cause unnecessary hardship or bloodshed? True, violent treatment is always a possibility for those who choose to resist, as has become obvious during the 2020 social justice protests concerning the killing of George Floyd. At times, to be treated violently cannot be avoided. But still, how can we be wise as serpents but gentle as doves? I will argue that the feet-on-the-ground praxis foundational to a badass Christianity is a faith that embraces hopelessness and implements acts of *jodiendo*—acts that f*ck with the social structures responsible for oppression.

Just as land throughout the Global South came to be occupied by European powers, so too are the minds of the original inhabitants of the land, for if their minds can be colonized, then the very physical and spiritual essence of their being becomes ripe for subjugation and domestication. White Christianity has for centuries constructed abstract philosophical and theological ideas that tickle the cerebrum in a vain attempt to reconcile the quest for liberty and justice among whites with their purposeful exclusion from the equation of those whom they deem inferior. This is not an issue of hypocrisy by whites spewing rhetoric about freedom and equality; instead, it is an attempt to theologically justify oppression through liberty-based platitudes. Moving religious discussion into the abstract effectively obscures the economic need to dispossess and disenfranchise the colonized and their descendants. Universal white celestial concepts of rights blind the dominant culture to the concrete realities of oppression at the hands of such freedom-voicing Euro-Americans. As this book has been arguing, all Eurocentric philosophical and religious thought is detrimental to the lives of the colonized and oppresses the world's disenfranchised. Our only hope of salvation is the total rejection of Eurocentric religious thought designed to maintain neoliberal structures.

If philosophical and theological thought is a particular cultural construct, then those born into and/or raised within the United States are a product of a society where white supremacy and class privilege have historically been interwoven with how whites, for centuries, see and organize the world around them. How they see has been legitimized as universal. These racist and classist underpinnings contribute to a metanarrative in which those within white culture develop their way of thinking. They construct a worldview in which complicity with Eurocentrism is normal and where those who benefit from white supremacy usually accept the present order of things, failing to consider the racialization of how they see and organize their world. Regardless of how alluring Eurocentric philosophy and theology might appear to the colonized, most of it remains embedded within white supremacy and thus is incongruent with any gospel message of liberation.

Nationalist Christians demonstrate this incongruency by believing whatever and whoever supports their exceptionalist worldview and elevated (even if delusional) station within society. Trump simply happens to be the vanilla flavor of the moment for this current generation. Even though white privilege is designed to empower a chosen 1 percent, and even though poor whites have economically more in common with communities of color than with middle-class whites, and even though the white middle class continues to be misused by fellow skinfolk benefiting from the social structures, most Euro-Americans continue to defend and excuse the 1 percent perpetrators responsible for abusing them economically. White minds are just as colonized as those of communities of color. Salvation as liberation will never materialize as long as whites and nonwhites continue to define reality through Eurocentric philosophical and theological concepts. The first act of any liberationist project must be to decolonize our own minds, which have been conditioned to see reality through the lens of the oppressors. Raising one's consciousness contributes to the decolonization of one's mind, hence the importance of books like this one.

Christianity was never about what one believes or professes but what one does. When we all finally get to walk through them pearly gates, we will discover how wrong we all were, realizing that our finite minds were never capable of grasping God's infinity. What we claim is true simply reflects the unexamined biases and errors with which we were raised. A contrite heart is outwardly manifested by what we actually do. Social ethics is not the mistake of the church;

it is the purpose of the church. To be badass means we do not remain philosophically true to some religious ideology but instead engage in acts that reflect a heart broken by the plight of the world's disenfranchised.

"Truly I tell you, whatever you did for one of the least of these siblings of mine, you did for me" (Matt. 25:40). Whatever you did—not whatever you believed, nor whatever you professed, nor wherever you worshiped, nor whomever you worshiped. Called to stand in solidarity with the hungry and thirsty, the naked and undocumented, the infirm and the incarcerated means more than simply providing charity—because even white Christians do this. Solidarity requires destabilizing the very social structures that institutionalize oppression so true liberation can flourish. Fulfilling Jesus's call to the least of these requires a badass Christianity that screws with power structures as a subversive praxis that might move us, as a society, closer to justice.

Commitment to a Radical Solidarity with the Oppressed

> [Badass Christianity is] . . . commitment to a radical solidarity with the oppressed, realizing that no one can ever be "saved" as long as the poor continue to be damned by our current economic structures.

Jesus does not stand in solidarity with the hungry and thirsty, the naked and undocumented, the infirm and incarcerated.

Jesus *is* the hungry and thirsty, the naked and undocumented, the infirm and incarcerated. It is we who are called to stand in radical solidarity with Jesus incarnated among the least of these as a praxis that assures humanity that no one—regardless of their race or ethnicity—stands alone in the presence of overwhelming oppressive social structures devised to rob the poor of the world of their dignity and personhood. This communal, radical solidarity can be implemented through the praxis of *acompañamiento*. Accompanying enfleshes a preferential option made for the oppressed. Walking alongside the least of these emphasizes the daily commitment to the communal "we" found within a God who took on flesh to accompany humanity in their daily struggle. "Because it is an option for particular flesh-and-blood persons," theologian Roberto Goizueta reminds us, "it will also be an option for particular *places*, the places where the poor live, die, and struggle for survival. To 'opt for the poor' is thus to place ourselves *there*, to *accompany* the poor person in his or her life, death, and struggle for survival."[36] To be accompanied by God, and in turn to accompany the least of these, restores the humanity, dignity, and worth of those relegated to nonperson status because they are nonwhite.

A badass Christianity accompanies Jesus down the *via dolorosa* as he makes his way to Calvary to die in radical solidarity accompanying all those being crucified today by white nationalist supremacy. To accompany the least of these is to accompany Jesus, which in turn means being accompanied by the Jesus who dies upon on the imperial crosses of power, profit, and privilege. Jesus and the least of these are neither abandoned nor alone because we choose *acompañamiento*, because we choose to accompany the disenfranchised in their struggle for an abundant life. Communal bonds to a God who also struggles and suffers alongside the least of these is reaffirmed by our radical solidarity of *acompañamiento*. In the midst of Good Friday's hopelessness, a glimmer of resurrection is present, which might just be enough to embolden and strengthen the least of these in their struggle to bring about overarching structural changes to death-causing policies justified and sustained by white Christianity.

Examples abound of groups embodying the radical act of *acompañamiento*. Think of the Sikh Center of New York. When New York City was in the early stages of becoming the epicenter of the coronavirus pandemic, the Sikh faithful fed the hungry by packaging over thirty thousand home-cooked meals for self-isolated Americans.[37] Or think of the hundreds of Egyptian Muslims who, during a time of religious strife in 2011, showed up for Coptic Christmas Eve mass and offered their bodies as human shields so that Christians, fearful for their safety and security, could worship in peace.[38] Or think of Southside Presbyterian Church in Tucson who, during the height of the US-backed killing fields in Central America, launched the 1980s sanctuary movement by opening its church doors to welcome aliens in our midst, saving immigrants from certain death.[39] These faith communities demonstrate how orthopraxis, not orthodoxy, is the key to being badass.

Celebration of Belief

> [Badass Christianity is] . . . celebration of belief through whichever cultural symbols best connect us to the Deity.

Those who are entering into their eternal rest that has been prepared for them since the foundation of the earth are not welcomed because they embraced a particular faith tradition; they are welcomed because they embraced a particular people—the least of these. Whiteness fails to see how the least of these is Jesus in the flesh. The white Jesus and the faith tradition that he represents, evangelized by Euro-Americans, is life-denying. To bend one's knee to the white Jesus means bending one's knee to white supremacy, the symbol of so much bloodletting among communities of color. This white Jesus is not detrimental solely to communities of color, robbing them of their humanity. White Jesus also brutalizes whites, who lose their humanity by following him.

What hope is there for whites who for generations followed a white Jesus who has stood for colonialism, slavery, manifest destiny, gunboat diplomacy, and all matter of oppressive political structures? Their only hope is to reject this cultural symbol they have used to understand divinity. Simply stated, whites need to get saved. They must crucify their white supremacy and their white theology in hope of a resurrection that would make them new creatures in the God of the oppressed. For those who claim Christianity, only the Black Jesus, or Jesús, or the queer Jesus, or any other representation of Jesus that emerges from the underside of whiteness, has the cosmic power to save and liberate. Just like communities of color, whites—for their own salvation and liberation—must learn to follow the Jesus of the dispossessed, the Jesus of the disenfranchised, the Jesus of the disinherited. This is not a call for political correctness but rather a call for *spiritual correctness*, a call to be born again—but not as white Christians.

Rejection of Laws and Regulations Made Mainly by Men

> [Badass Christianity is] . . . rejection of laws and regulations made mainly by men, specifically white men, which trespass upon the basic rights of all.

Bodies of color have existed under authoritarian, nondemocratic, white rule that tells them where they can live, where they can work, where they can study, and where they can take a dump. People of color may have bled in every military conflict in which the United States fought to secure liberty, but they mainly shed their blood to keep whites free. White religious and political institutions, which for many centuries have sustained white privilege, cannot be trusted to expand the ideals of liberty to communities of color. Martin Luther King Jr., in his 1963 letter from a Birmingham Jail, reminds us that "freedom is never voluntarily given by the oppressor; it must be demanded by the oppressed." But I wonder whether the word "demanded" might be too timid a response. What good are our demands if they continue to be ignored? Aldous Huxley might be closer to the necessary praxis when he states: "Liberties aren't given, they are taken."

True, there have been brief moments when the dominant culture, believing in their own rhetoric, proactively stood on the right side of history. For example, during the Civil Rights era the US higher court system was at times an ally in the struggle for racial justice. But such institutions, which were once open to demands for justice, were easily co-opted to advance the tenets of white supremacy as we see by the restructuring of the federal court system's ethos since 2016. Not only was a Supreme Court seat literally stolen from Obama for this purpose, but vacancies on the appellate bench were filled with decisively unqualified Trump appointees—seats kept vacant by the Republican Senate, who refused to confirm the nominated justices of the previous administration.

As I have written elsewhere, we have evolved into a society that must go to the police department to get a permit from the police department to protest against the police department about its police brutality. Freedom to protest is protected but overly processed. We can always drive to a march. We can carry signs and shout slogans so long as we do not disrupt the social equilibrium designed to protect the unearned power, profit, and privilege of the few. Protest is allowed so long as the social equilibrium justified by the religious leaders of the prevailing nationalist Christianity is not threatened. We have domesticated protest, tamed rebellion, normalized opposition, and capitalized and merchandised it all. Through social media we can express with a stroke on our keypads a moral outrage that costs us nothing and changes even less. Activism has become cheap and ineffective. If the goal is to bring about liberative change, then we must move beyond rules legislated and implemented by the dominant white nationalist culture.

A white theology had to be created to limit who is called for liberation and, by extension, salvation. Eurocentric theology and politics were formulated to exclude and blame the colonized for their inability to participate in the national rhetoric of freedom and liberty. When citizens of the United States speak of its long, proud tradition of democracy, they are not lying, but democracy was limited to white folk. For Native people on the reservation, for African Americans in the Jim and Jane Crow South, for Latinx folks throughout the Southwest, and for all other minorities, living under authoritarian, fatal white rule was always the norm throughout US history—a history whose residue remains visible to this day in the white majority's laws and legislations. Communities of color self-discipline, as if interned in a panopticon, whenever they continue to follow laws and legislation enacted to protect and expand white supremacy. Liberation has always required disobeying laws and legislation designed for the demise of the disenfranchised.

Survival Ethics

> [Badass Christianity is] . . . a survival ethics that responds to the hopelessness of the people.

What do you do when the God of liberation, who is proclaimed from the depths of marginalization, fails to liberate? How do we maintain faith when God's promises fall short in the face of decimation? Vague calls for hope allow listeners to hear in the message their own desires and expectations. Hope minus action equals spiritual hypocrisy. Hope that all things will eventually work for good for those called by God's name (see Rom. 8:28) fosters a lazy praxis. In the face of repressive social structures repudiating all Jesus taught, white Christianity creates middle-class hope to satisfy any urge to take action toward social change. Among Eurocentric Christians, a theology of hope may sound liberative but, I argue, it actually reinforces oppression of the colonized.

Eurocentric hope is not some wishful optimistic desire

but a joyful expectation that God will bring about God's perfect purposes. Jürgen Moltmann, the prophet of hope, argues for hope because he places his faith on a God who keeps promises. Moltmann's hope is especially attractive to whites because, in spite of life's difficulties, they can hope in a God whose promises validate the good news, who assures the reward of eternal life, who provides meaning and purpose to the future, and who fortifies a sense of security, a sense of peace, and a tranquility of the mind in the midst of trials and tribulations.[40] But what if you are a person of color? What if annihilation still awaits the faithful regardless of the hope they possess or profess? Such hope becomes an imposition upon bodies of color. The least of these who represent the poor, the oppressed, and the colonized of the world live their lives where first world promises of hope are not necessarily apparent. Hope saves white Christianity from having to wrestle with how their power, privilege, and profits are directly linked to the dispossession and disenfranchisement of the least of these. So long as white Christians can embrace hope, they can wash their hands of their complicity with the human virus responsible for the deadly racist structures they have designed. They can remain locked down in gated communities, snug in their illusion that God will somehow take care of the least of these, so that they, as white nationalist Christians, need not.

White Christians may very well be an Easter Sunday

people, but those relegated to their margins are a Holy Saturday people. The least of these occupy the liminal in-between space, where the gore and brutality of Friday's crucifixion and the not-yet resurrection of Sunday's Easter are constant companions. In this ambiguous space, some faint good news is easily trodden down by everyday realities. To sit in the radical solidarity of Saturday is to discover how hope falls short, reduced to an opioid used to numb us from the pain of Friday and drug us from effectively implementing radical liberative praxis.[41] Hope domesticates. So long as the least of these have something to lose, they will police themselves from engaging in liberative praxis. Think of the sign at the entrance to Auschwitz, *Arbeit macht frei*. This lie created enough hope among the condemned to stifle attempts to rebel. The promise of hope of survival is the strongest component in maintaining oppressive structures. Only when the least of these realize that they have nothing to lose, that they are already dead bodies walking, can they become the most dangerous to those seeking to prop up universal norms. Contrary to Moltmann, hopelessness is not the despair of rolling into a fetal position and gnashing one's teeth. Hopelessness is the desperation that propels the marginalized with nothing to lose toward praxis. Hope may soothe white Christians with easy, quick solutions or reliance on divine miracles, but it is no alternative for constructing a more just social arrangement.[42]

Liberation of All

> [Badass Christianity is] . . . a liberation and salvation dis-
> covered as one's struggle with others for the liberation of all.

Unease with communities of color because they are not
white enough or sufficiently assimilated to the wolves' understanding of God is infused with a heavy dose of xenophobic, misogynist, or hateful tendencies. This hatred unites a
people behind politicians promising to fix their problems, to
make them great again. Regardless of whether the economic
policies these politicians advocate are beneficial or whether
the politicians have opportunities to place people from their
own political party in high government posts, complicity remains a rejection of the gospel message. Because nationalist
Christians voted in 2016 and 2020 to again trump the gospel
with political expedience, such a Christianity must whole-
heartedly be rejected. For goats to be saved they need to approach the throne with broken and contrite hearts, weeping
for their complicity in slaughtering sheep to be devoured by
hungry wolves of means.

Although white Christianity is neither monolithic nor
uniform, it has certain common characteristics, specifically
(1) a predilection for hyperindividualism; (2) a demand for
"law and order"; (3) an emphasis on personal charity over and
against public justice-building; (4) an acceptance that God's
will is reflected in neoliberalism and market economics; and

(5) an emphasis on an orthodoxy based on deductive thinking over and against an orthopraxis based on inductive reasoning. These proclivities are what makes white Christianity so damning to communities of color. And no matter how hard people of color attempt to assimilate, they will never be fully accepted because they are, after all, of color. Communities of color seeking assimilation must first circumcise their culture and identity to embrace white Christianity, a cut demanded by the dominant culture that forces a denial of the gospel mandate concerning the hungry, thirsty, and naked. The only way people of color can become ontologically white is by joining them in ignoring the cry and presence of the least of these.

Rejection of Eurocentric Theological Thought

> [Badass Christianity is] . . . rejection of Eurocentric theological thought due to its colonizing, philosophical world view.

Supreme Court justice Clarence Thomas, in a documentary released in 2020, claims that the true Klansmen are the liberals.[43] Thomas is ontologically white. People of color who support the current nationalist Christian establishment suffer from colonized minds that see reality through the eyes of white cisgender males. But this is nothing new, for there have always been agents of white supremacy, traitors to their own race or ethnicity—whether they be Indian scouts leading the cavalry to massacre fellow Native people or capos in prison camps carrying out the whims of sadistic guards in hopes of surviving a few extra days. This desperation to survive or the greed to personally benefit motivated many throughout the centuries to become coerced or willing agents of white supremacy. At times, some of these agents really came to believe the lies lifted up by whiteness, becoming willing participants in the destruction, usually through assimilation, of their own people.

Once minds are colonized, bodies can be controlled with little effort. The search is always on to find faces of color with white voices who are willing to be placed upon pedestals to defend white supremacy. And if those voices also embrace a nationalist Christianity, so much the better. Creators of white Christian thought legitimize a way of being and thinking in which occupied minds produce the illusion of liberated bodies. Free citizens of color are mentally shackled when they become subjected to a faith that justifies privilege as God's will and legitimizes power in the hands of the few as God's design. Sniveling predators wearing priestly vestments carve a space within power structures for themselves by fawning over political opportunists. In return for their support of the white establishment, they receive the opportunity to get their message out—a message that contributes to the colonization of the minds of those who share their skin pigmentation, ethnicity, language, or locale. They often appear on race-based outlets like Fox News as white-appointed spokespersons for their communities of color. Brown-nosing can even procure invitations to the Oval Office to lay hands upon the one committed to a nationalist Christianity. The ruthless and cruel who devour the innocent mask their agency to white supremacy under cloaks of piety, appearing as Indigenous angels of light. But the white-bred Christianity they proclaim ravishes the least of these as these Brown agents of white supremacy grow wealthy off the mite of the Latina widow. They leave nothing to the imagination but the advancement and expansion of a violator's grasp. Their deep-throated support is rewarded with opportunities to offer prayers at the inauguration of a racist president.

Samuel Rodriguez, who created the National Hispanic Leadership Conference, has provided political cover for Trump's heartless immigration policies among Latinx people, even though he claims he is trying to be a voice for the undocumented. He is delusional if he believes that a president who captured the highest office in the land by beginning his campaign with anti-immigrant rhetoric would even be interested in hearing a voice from that community. Regardless of whether Rodriguez repents from the sin of placing his trust in Trump rather than in the Lamb, his sin is not in the asininity of being deceived by an avowed racist who partly made his fortune through redlining but by willingly participating in colonizing the minds of others. Rodriguez embraces a white nationalist Christianity that is and always will be detrimental to the community he claims to represent.

Naively seeking to solve the issue of race, Rodriguez employs the hyper-individuality of white Christianity by claiming the answer is not found through political advocacy but through repentance of a personal sin whose absolution is found when one becomes born-again (code language for becoming born-again into white Christianity). He preaches that racism is not a hate problem but a heart problem.[44] Let us be clear—racism is and always has been a hate problem. For those who doubt that racism is a hate problem, may I humbly suggest they speak to those of us who have experienced the physical violence this hatred engendered? Rodriguez's theology, as well as that of his fellow ontologically white Latino evangelicals (such as Mario Bramnick, Pasqual Urrabazo, and Ramiro Peña) who also have deep ties to Trump, reinforces a white Christianity because it reduces all attempts to bring about racial and ethnic justice to a matter of prayer rather than praxis. Brown ministers' colonized minds lead them into believing any demonstration of intelligence on their part can be achieved only through white Christian academic paradigms. But as we have already seen, the particularity of white intellectual and spiritual thought poses a danger to those seeking liberation for their minds. Unfortunately, scholars of color with liberative inclinations have, more often than not, looked toward oppressors for the means of defining and expressing their thoughts, a fact easily verified by scrutinizing the Eurocentric-based footnotes in the writings of early liberation theologians. We seek to explain how to liberate dark bodies through white thinkers. We attempt to add some tokenized color to white ideals in hopes of humanizing those same white thinkers who dehumanize us. More insidious than controlling bodies through hunger, thirst, and nakedness is the control of their minds.

Each new generation born into Eurocentric domination has been taught, since childhood, to see and interpret reality through white eyes. Worse, they learn to see and define their identity by how whites defined them to justify the rape, theft, and enslavement of their bodies. Their very being must be defined as less-than to justify exploitation. As a religious worldview, white Christianity must be legitimized and normalized to morally and spiritually defend the undefendable. Darker bodies of color must be kept hungry, thirsty, and naked to validate the supremacy of whiteness and vindicate neoliberal advances, which continue to contribute to their unmerited power, profit, and privilege. The colonization of the minds of those defined as falling short of whiteness is proven successful when they learn to define their own bodies, consciously or unconsciously, through Eurocentric philosophical, theological, or theoretical paradigms.

Sadly, these ministers with Brown faces but speaking with white voices lead many of their people to vote against their own best interests. That 33 percent of Latinx Protestants approve and support a racist president who kicked off his presidential campaign by demonizing Brown bodies is problematic. That 11 percent of Latinx Protestants say there is nothing Trump can do—nothing—that would cause them to waver on their support for him is colonial brainwashing on a massive scale.[45] But Brown spokespersons for whiteness serve a more important purpose than simply attempting to produce converts from within their own community. They provide cover and permission for white Christians to support anti-Latinx policies with peace of mind, proving they aren't racist because they can point to a Brown face who mimics a kinder, gentler version of their white venom.

The decolonization of our minds begins with the full and total rejection of white Christianity and all those within our community who, for monetary rewards, or access to positions in power, or colonized minds, peddle its lies. The task of decolonization of our minds begins with learning to think our own thoughts rooted within our own communities of color, apart from white Eurocentrism. No person can serve two masters, for they will love one and despise the other (see Matt. 6:24). Any colonized person who serves and loves white Christianity, which was created to spiritually justify their exclusion, or the white gods and Jesuses bent on their subservience will learn how to despise the religious and philosophical wisdom embedded within their own community.

Disruptive and Revolutionary

> [Badass Christianity is] . . . disruptive and revolutionary,
> overturning the temple's tables of oppressors.

Nationalist Christianity will remain firmly in place, detrimental not only to communities of color but also to white communities, until tables are overturned. White Christians who obtained or inherited their unearned power, profit, and privilege through violence visited upon bodies of color piously demand that any attempts to create a more just society must occur nonviolently and according to a plan controlled by and within their oversight. They fail to recognize how their societal positions are due to kaleidoscopic forms of institutionalized violence. The political structures they created are vicious, literally bringing the lives of the marginalized to an early death. To maintain the institutional violence furthering the occupation of the minds of communities of color, white Christians tell the oppressed they must obtain their liberation through peaceful and appropriate means.

But on what moral authority can the perpetrator of centuries of violence dictate terms by which the oppressed are to achieve their liberation? White Christian nationalists point to a Jesus who they say is a pacifist but continue in the not-so-private public sphere to worship the warrior Jesus, the one celebrated in the song "Onward Christian Soldiers." Even white pacifists, with the best of intentions, remain complicit with oppression. Howard Yoder may have envisioned a non-violent white Mennonite when he wrote *The Politics of Jesus* (even though he was extremely violent toward women[46]), but such a Jesus is not biblically accurate.

Jesus, the so-called pacifist, responds to institutionalized violence by walking into the center of power, weaving a whip, overturning tables, and physically chasing out the bankers who are economically oppressing the poor (see John 3:15). He advises his disciples, as they set out on their missionary ventures, that if they lack a sword, to "sell their cloak and purchase one" (Luke 22:35-36). Buy a sword—let that sink in as you hear the ideology of a pacifist Jesus being defended. Buying a sword back then is equivalent to buying a gun now. When Jesus was arrested at the Garden of Gethsemane, Peter impetuously drew his sword and cut off the ear of a slave belonging to the High Priest. What is a disciple of a pacifist doing with a sword? Jesus's response may have been, "All those who take the sword perish from the sword" (Matt. 26:52), but to whom was he directing his comments? After all, earlier that night when his disciples bragged about having two swords by which to defend him (see Luke 22:38), Jesus does not rebuke them. If his comment concerning Peter's impulsive act was directed at his disciples, then he would be contradicting himself, for as we have seen, the idea to buy a sword was his in the first place. His comments were directed to those who came to arrest him.

Those who pick up the sword in defense of empire will, with the empire, perish by the sword.

Jesus may very well abhor violence, as I do—but that does not automatically make us pacifists. We do not advocate violence because oppressors, privileged by the government, have all the guns, along with the full support of the police and the military. So do white supremacist groups! For communities of color to employ violence is tactically suicidal. Employing violence in the search for liberation gives defenders of white supremacy an excuse to unleash all the police powers and military might at their disposal. This is why I find the words of César Chávez so relevant: "I am not a nonviolent man. I am a violent man who is trying to be nonviolent."[47] For those of us who grew up on mean streets—made mean by centuries of institutionalized violence—the lesson we soon learned is that pacifism seldom works in the schoolyard. In the messiness of adult life, the ideal of nonviolence actually increases the violence that has been institutionalized by oppressors, who may loudly denounce unjust social structures but will never abdicate their birthright to power or profits thanks to white affirmative action. The dominant culture, including progressive Christians, may be willing to offer charity or make a show of standing in solidarity with people of color, but few are willing or able to take an active and decisive role in dismantling the very global structures designed to privilege them at the expense of the world's majority.

The violence we use to overcome oppression is in reality an effort to defend ourselves from the institutionalized violence already bleeding us dry. A preferential option for the oppressed means standing over and against their oppressors who hold a vested interest in violently protecting what they perceive is theirs. Within the social structures that for centuries have used institutional violence to keep opponents of white supremacy in check, maybe it's time for a conversation among the oppressed. Is it time to weave whips in defense of the disenfranchised? This is a conversation in which whites hold no moral authority to participate. Unless as a culture we begin to move toward a more equitable society where liberty and justice are indeed for all, the specter of violence and the fear it induces among whites will continue during the reigns of future Trumps.

Calling Bullshit

> [Badass Christianity is] . . . calling bullshit on religious and political hypocrisy.

Some are saying the Trump era is a wake-up call for Christians. Some are saying Christians will rise up against this injustice. Some are saying this is the last straw. I call bullshit. The major problem concerning the oppression faced by people of color is the religious apologists for racism. More is required than just signing another damn petition usually read only by the signers themselves in order to see who else added their names to the cause. Jesus is again arrested, imprisoned, and crucified by the clerics of empire, who for thirty pieces of silver made a bargain to have a say in packing the federal court system. It becomes the responsibility of communities of color to wrestle Jesus from the hands of those with hearts of stone. To be a badass Christian—heck, to be a human being—requires us to turn over the tables of the money-changing and profit-making Homeland Security system, as well as the so-called Justice Department defending unjust activities. Politicians have set up shop in God's holy temple. We must weave whips to drive out the anti-Latinx hymn-singers who remain complicit with violence. Every church and seminary must become a sanctuary house—if not, they should be converted into museums, tourist sites, country clubs, or banks. Every religious organization must defend the least of these in open rebellion against the injustices of a racist government's desire to crush the marginalized under their rhetoric of life, liberty, and the pursuit of happiness. Every minister who refuses to be thrown into the colosseum to face the lions of the new Rome for standing in solidarity with the oppressed should hang up their collar, for that minister is of no use to God or God's creation. Every Latinx person must register to vote and then vote against politicians who continue to see us, or our siblings of color, as less than human—regardless if we agree on other hot-button cultural issues. Every white person who insists they are color-blind should go buy some prescription glasses. Every white person who voted for Trump must repent before a holy God for crying out before Pilate, "Caesar is lord." Every white person who wants to be an ally should refuse to speak for us but instead assist us in amplifying our voices. Every Christian who refuses to stand in solidarity with Jesus incarnated as Jesús the alien, who is trying to emerge from the shadows to which immigration policies have relegated him, should consider getting saved. And when a nationalist Christianity dares to impose their satanic doctrines masked as biblical truth upon a people, with one voice we must rise up and declare that truth—bullshit!

Costly—Sacrificing All

> [Badass Christianity is] . . . costly—sacrificing all, even one's life or security, for the sake of justice.

For several years I have been an advocate for what I have been calling an ethics *para joder*, an ethics "that f*cks with." Before the vastness of institutionalized racism, institutionalized violence, and institutionalized oppression, where resistance is indeed futile and victory over evil is hopeless, the only response is an ethics *para joder*, an ethics that "screws" with the prevailing power structures. Few alternatives exist for the least of these to use to demand justice. They can always hope white Christians might have a come to Jesus moment and crucify their privilege, but until now, such hope has accomplished little to lift the burden of centuries of oppression. Few liberals and progressives are willing to lift a finger if it entails being stripped of their white affirmative action. Full frontal rebellion often leads to massacres whenever white affirmative action is threatened. How then can change be brought forth without people of color becoming martyrs? F*cking with the power structures becomes a badass Christian tactic. If law and order maintain oppressive structures, then subversion provides opportunities for new strategies to arise.

To *joder* is to consciously become a pain in the ass of the powerful, to purposely cause trouble for the privileged, to constantly disrupt the established norm of the profiters. To *joder* is to shout from the mountain top that which oppressors prefer to be kept silent. The *joderon* audaciously refuses to stay in their place. When marginalized communities begin to *joder*, the prevailing power structures are threatened and disabled. To *joder* is a subversive praxis that refuses to play by the rules established by those who maintain social order because it protects their privilege, power, and profit. If the goal is to bring forth a just society, which, by definition, means that the current unjust one must be overthrown, then no choice exists but to move beyond established rules designed to maintain the current system.

Let Jesus be our example. When he overturned bankers' tables, he was *jodiendo*. This badass ethics of *jodiendo* is not some new concept dreamed up in my ivory tower, for this has always been a survival strategy employed by the world's wretched. Coining the neologism an ethics *para joder* simply puts into words a practice that has existed for centuries. As an organic intellectual, I am simply taking a page from our cultures of color and embracing the trickster image. Consider the coyote and the spider within the Indigenous community, or br'er rabbit within the African American community, or Cantinflas within the Mexican community, or Elegúa within my own Cuban community—all tricksters who, through lies, humor, tricks, and tomfoolery, unmasked the hypocrisies of the dominating oppressors. How does one ethically lie to discover truth and morally steal to feed the hungry? Can we even dare ask to virtuously kill to save lives?

Think of the slaveholder in the antebellum South who hires a preacher to teach his slaves not to steal, to work hard, and to obey their master as unto the Lord. The one who stole the slave's body in the first place establishes the rule that defines stealing, laziness, or disobedience as illegal or immoral. An ethics *para joder* would argue that slaves have a moral obligation to steal from the master's coop to feed their families, to pretend to work hard while trying to conserve as much energy as possible so as to survive, to disobey, and when possible, to free themselves. The laws that reinforced the white Christianity of that time were not only satanic but had to be overcome and overpowered. Unfortunately, those slavocracy norms simply morphed into what we have today.

Last Gasp or Renewed Resurgence?

The election of Barack Obama may have provided hope that "yes, we can," but Euro-American nationalist Christianity firmly responded "no, you can't" with the election of Donald Trump. The election of a Black man in 2008 was a wake-up call to a white nation accustomed to its place in the world. Immediate race-based pushback took form in the "birther" movement spearheaded by Trump. Additionally, the Tea Party movement contributed to electoral victories in the 2010 midterm elections. But with Obama's reelection in 2012, a lost America hollered from the mountaintops.

Today, the nation finds itself at a crossroad. Are we witnesses to the last gasp of a Christian nation steeped in white supremacy? Will the rejection of Christianity by Millennials and Generation Z usher in the demise of a white Christianity that has misappropriated the teachings of Jesus? Politically, the demise of the mainstream Republican Party, which once emphasized fiscal responsibility, makes future electoral victories unsustainable—even untenable, because it is committed to be the party of white men in an era of demographic change. After Mitt Romney's 2012 defeat, the Republican National Committee conducted a study that concluded that if the party failed to reach out to people of color, women, and youth, it was destined to political extinction, unable to win future elections.[48] But rather than beginning to make itself more inclusive, the Republican Party instead turned toward the nativist ideology of Trump in the next presidential election. Defeat of nationalist Christianity may have been delayed, but it cannot be forever postponed, unless we move away from democratic principles. Political manipulative falsehoods over persuasion can go only so far.

We may very well be witnessing both the Republican Party's and white Christianity's decision to stay white as an act of suicide as it more tightly embraces the antichrist of our age. But then again, this is not the first time the Christianity of oppressors embraced antichrists. And probably it will not be the last. This may very well be the last gasp of a white supremacy in Christian nationalist garb, or it could just as likely be the resurgence of a new form of apartheid, a reorganizing of society so that the future white minority can retain power and be protected by sharpening the rule of law in their favor. Trump may very well have been a useful tool for those among the white elite hoping to restructure society for their benefit. Regardless of whether we are witnessing a last gasp or a renewed resurgence, one thing is for sure: white Christian ethical incompetence and moral negligence concerning Trump and their employment of the biblical text to justify public policies and personal behaviors mean they can never again say anything concerning justice or righteousness. If they do, they would not be taken seriously. They have lost all moral authority to say anything about anything.

A Final Note

This manuscript was finished in the spring of 2020. Who knows whether you are reading this book during Trump's second term, or if he served only one term and someone else is now in office, or if he is serving a third term after spearheading a change to the Constitution, or if he is still serving after suspending elections for some excuse? Who knows? But whatever the future brings, one thing is certain—Trump, at the end of the day, is irrelevant. Like all humans, he will return to the ground from which we all arose to become food for the worms. What truly matters is not Trump but the future of Christianity, specifically the white Christianity that was refashioned in his own image. The issue was never Trump but rather how he steered whites in this nation to the point of no return, where they were unable to whiff the stench of white Christianity's rotting corpse. Regardless of whether he wins or loses the 2020 presidential election, his fervent supporters will feel only rage and fear about those whom they have oppressed and repressed over the centuries. I suspect this fear and rage will support a deeper level of despair requiring a more militant response. Feeling betrayed by their own government, which no longer champions their white affirmative action or secures an assured space from which they are supposed to rule over the least of these, white Christians are probably the greatest threat to democracy.

What the era of Trump has successfully accomplished has been to reinforce and heighten white anxiety. We have lost the opportunity to explore the possibilities of a more multicultural, justice-based social order in which all can participate and enjoy its fruits. Because diversity was made into a threat rather than a solution, the future is indeed bleak. But there is another possibility. We can come together, learn how to live together peacefully and without racism, and share in the nation's resources. Unfortunately, the apex of the Trump administration has made me hopeless. Let's hope I'm wrong.

Notes

Chapter 1

1. James H. Cone, *A Black Theology of Liberation* (Maryknoll, NY: Orbis Books, 2010 [1970]), 10.

2. Jessica Martínez and Gregory A. Smith, "How the Faithful Voted: A Preliminary 2016 Analysis," Pew Research Center, November 9, 2016, https://www.pewresearch.org/fact-tank/2016/11/09/how-the-faithful-voted-a-preliminary-2016-analysis/.

3. Daniel Cox and Robert P. Jones, "America's Changing Religious Identity: Findings from the 2016 American Values Atlas," Public Religion Research Institute, September 6, 2017, https://www.prri.org/research/american-religious-landscape-christian-religiously-unaffiliated/.

4. Annie Karni, "At CPAC, Trump Takes Aim at Rivals," *The New York Times*, February 29, 2020.

5. Meagan Flynn, "Trump's Spiritual Adviser Seeks His Protection from 'Demonic Networks' at Reelection Rally," *The Washington Post*, June 19, 2019.

Chapter 2

1. Jeremy Diamond, "Trump: I Could 'Shoot Somebody and I Wouldn't Lose Votes,'" CNN, January 24, 2016.

2. "By a Narrow Margin, Americans Say Senate Trial Should Result in Trump's Removal," Pew Research Center, January 22, 2020.

3. "Fractured Nation: Widening Partisan Polarization and Key Is-

sues in 2020 Presidential Elections," Public Religion Research Institute, October 20, 2019.

4. "Fractured Nation."

5. Josh Dawsey and Sarah Pulliam Bailey, "Trump Rages at Christian Magazine That Called Him 'Grossly Immoral,' but Still Finds Evangelical Support," *The Washington Post*, December 20, 2019.

6. "White Evangelicals See Trump as Fighting for Their Beliefs, Though Many Have Mixed Feelings about His Personal Conduct," Pew Research Center, March 12, 2020.

7. David Crary, "'Deeply Problematic,' Faith Leaders Express Concern over Trump's Political Attacks at National Prayer Breakfast," *Time*, February 6, 2020.

8. Crary, "'Deeply Problematic.'"

9. Kevin M. Kruse, *One Nation under God: How Corporate America Invented Christian America* (New York: Basic Books, 2015), 6–8.

10. Darren Dochuk, "The Other Brother Duo That Brought Us the Modern GOP," *Politico*, September 2, 2019.

11. Kruse, *One Nation under God*, 17–18.

12. Kruse, *One Nation under God*, 11.

13. Kruse, *One Nation under God*, 36.

14. Kruse, *One Nation under God*, 256, 262.

15. Deal W. Hudson, *Onward, Christian Soldiers: The Growing Political Power of Catholics and Evangelicals in the United States* (New York: Threshold Editions, 2008), 15.

16. Marc J. Ambinder, "Inside the Council for National Policy," *ABC News*, May 2, 2001; David Von Drehle, "Social Conservatives' Ties to GOP Fraying," *The Washington Post*, February 28, 1999.

17. Frank Lambert, *Religion in American Politics: A Short History* (Princeton: Princeton University Press, 2008), 224.

18. Jerry Falwell, "Massive Spiritual Aggression: A 21st Century Call to Action," sermon given at Thomas Road Baptist Church, Lynchburg, Virginia, May 1, 2005.

19. Rick Perlstein, "Exclusive: Lee Atwater's Infamous 1981 Interview on the Southern Strategy," *The Nation*, November 13, 2012.

20. David Nyhan, "New Right Leaders Cut Teeth in 60's," *Boston Globe*, February 17, 1981; Megan Rosenfeld, "Reining in the Right," *The Washington Post*, May 19, 1981.

21. David D. Kirkpatrick, "Club of the Most Powerful," *The New York Times*, August 28, 2004; David Von Drehle, "Social Conservatives' Ties to GOP Fraying Weyrich's Disillusion 'Touched a Chord,'" *The Washington Post*, February 28, 1999.

22. Lambert, *Religion in American Politics*, 224.

23. Jeremy Leaming, "Behind Closed Doors: Who Is the Council for National Policy and What Are They Up To? And Why Don't They Want You to Know?," *Church & State* 57, no. 9 (October 2004): 8–12.

24. Russ Bellant, *The Coors Connection: How Coors Family Philanthropy Undermines Democratic Pluralism* (Cambridge, MA: South End Press, 1991), 2; Leaming, "Behind Closed Doors," 8–12; Ambinder, "Inside the Council for National Policy"; Kirkpatrick, "Club of the Most Powerful."

25. Mark Mazzetti and Adam Goldman, "Erik Prince Recruits Ex-Spies to Help Infiltrate Liberal Groups," *The New York Times*, March 7, 2020.

26. http://www.publiceye.org/ifas/cnp/index.html; Kirkpatrick, "Club of the Most Powerful"; Leaming, "Behind Closed Doors"; Nan Levinson, *Outspoken: Free Speech Stories* (Berkeley: University of California Press, 2003), 203; D. Michael Lindsay, *Faith in the Halls of Power: How Evangelicals Joined the American Elite* (New York: Oxford University Press, 2007), 59.

27. Kirkpatrick, "Club of the Most Powerful."

28. Eduardo Porter, "Why America Will Never Get Medicare for All," *The New York Times*, March 15, 2020.

29. Stephen S. Lim et al., "Measuring Human Capital: A Systematic Analysis of 195 Countries and Territories, 1990–2016," *The Lancet* 392, no. 10154 (October 6, 2018): 1217–34.

30. Drew Desilver, "US Students' Academic Achievement Still Lags That of Their Peers in Many Other Countries," Pew Research Center, February 15, 2017.

31. Mark Abadi, "Income Inequality Is Growing across the US—Here's How Bad It Is in Every State," *Business Insider*, March 15, 2018.

32. Gerard F. Anderson, Peter Hussey, and Varduhi Petrosyan, "It's Still the Price, Stupid: Why the US Spends So Much on Health Care, and a Tribute to Uwe Reinhardt," *Health Affairs* 38, no. 1 (January 2019): 87–95.

33. Jorge L. Ortiz, "'A Distinctly American Phenomenon': Our Workforce Is Dying Faster Than Any Other Wealthy Country, Study Shows," *USA Today*, November 26, 2019.

34. Paul Weyrich, address at the Religious Right gathering, Dallas, Fall 1980, https://www.youtube.com/watch?v=8GBAsFwPglw.

35. Daniel Cox and Robert P. Jones, "America's Changing Religious Identity: Findings from the 2016 American Values Atlas," Public Religion Research Institute, September 6, 2017.

36. Aaron Blake, "Trump Just Comes Out and Says It: The GOP Is Hurt When It's Easier to Vote," *The Washington Post*, March 30, 2020.

37. David Jackson, "'Human Scum': Donald Trump Has Harsh Comments for 'Never Trumper' Republicans," *USA Today*, October 23, 2019.

38. Jonathan Allen, "Trump, Launching Re-Election Bid, Says Democrats 'Want to Destroy Our Country,'" NBC News, June 18, 2019.

39. Felicia Sonmez, "Trump Again Jokes about Staying on as President for More Than Two Terms," *The Washington Post*, April 18, 2019.

40. Benjy Sarlin, "Donald Trump Warns Supporters Could Riot If He Doesn't Get GOP Nomination," NBC News, March 17, 2016.

41. Trip Gabriel, "Donald Trump's Call to Monitor Polls Raises Fears of Intimidation," *The New York Times*, October 18, 2016.

42. Michael Crowley, "Trump's Long Dalliance with Violent Rhetoric," *Politico*, August 10, 2016.

43. Jeff Zeleny and Kevin Liptak, "Trump Warns Evangelicals of 'Violence' If GOP Loses in the Midterms," CNN, August 28, 2019.

44. Katie Shepherd and Brittany Shammas, "'Beyond Repugnant': GOP Congressman Slams Trump for Warning of 'Civil War' over Impeachment," *The Washington Post*, September 20, 2019.

45. Jerry H. Goldfeder and Lincoln Mitchell, "A Donald Trump Coup If He Loses in 2020? With All the Norms He's Busted, Don't Rule It Out," *USA Today*, March 14, 2019.

46. "In US, Decline of Christianity Continues at Rapid Pace: An Update on America's Changing Religious Landscape," Pew Research Center, October 17, 2019.

47. "Fractured Nation."

48. Christina Wilkie and Kevin Breuninger, "Trump Says He Told Pence Not to Call Governors Who Aren't 'Appreciative' of White House Coronavirus Efforts," CNBC News, March 27, 2020.

49. Ferdinand Saussure, *Course in General Linguistics*, ed. Charles Bally and Albert Sechehaye, trans. Wade Baskin (New York: Philosophical Library, 1959), 66–67.

50. Michel Foucault, *The Order of Things: An Archaeology of the Human Sciences* (New York: Vintage Books, 1994), 34.

51. Kate Benner, "Religious Freedom Training by Justice Dept. Raises Red Flag for Lawyers," *The New York Times*, March 14, 2020.

52. Jessica Glenza, "The Multimillion-Dollar Christian Group Attacking LGBTQ+ Rights," *The Guardian*, February 21, 2020.

53. Unless otherwised noted, all biblical translations are those of the author from the original Hebrew or Greek.

54. Sara Diamond, *Spiritual Warfare: The Politics of the Christian Right* (Boston: South End Press, 1989), 138, emphasis original.

55. John Fea, "Ted Cruz's Campaign Is Fueled by a Dominionist Vision for America," *The Washington Post*, February 4, 2016.

56. "Fractured Nation."

57. "Fractured Nation."

Chapter 3

1. Fernandra Santos and Rebekah Zemansky, "Arizona's Desert Swallows Migrants on Riskier Trails," *The New York Times*, May 20, 2013.

2. Jon Swaine and Juweek Adolphe, "Violence in the Name of Trump," *The Guardian*, August 28, 2019.

3. Jason Wilson, "US Hate Groups Have Seen Ideas Enter Mainstream in Trump Era, Report Finds," *The Guardian*, February 20, 2019.

4. Brad Brooks, "Victims of Anti-Latino Hate Crimes Soar in U.S.: FBI Report," *Reuters*, November 12, 2019.

5. Domenico Montanaro, "Trump Returns to Campaign Trail with a Familiar Message in a Changing World," NPR, June 20, 2020.

6. Knvul Sheikh and Roni Caryn Rabin, "The Coronavirus: What Scientists Have Learned So Far," *The New York Times*, March 10, 2020.

7. Andrea Barrera, "Mexico Reports Its Sixth Case of Coronavirus," *U.S. News & World Report*, March 6, 2020.

8. "Coronavirus: Mexicans Demand Crackdown on Americans Crossing the Border," BBC News, March 28, 2020.

9. Trip Gabriel, "Ohio Lawmaker Asks Racist Question about Black People and Hand-Washing," *The New York Times*, June 11, 2020.

10. Christopher Sherman, Martha Mendoza, and Garance Burke, "US Held Record Number of Migrant Children in Custody in 2019," Associated Press, November 12, 2019.

11. Quoted in Sherman, Mendoza, and Burke, "US Held Record Number of Migrant Children in Custody in 2019."

12. Julia Ainsley, "Trump Admin's 'Tent Cities' Cost More Than Keeping Migrant Kids with Parents," NBC News, June 20, 2018.

13. Manny Fernandez, "Lawyer Draws Outrage for Defending Lack of Toothbrushes in Border Detention," *The New York Times*, June 25, 2019.

14. Maya Rhodan, "Donald Trump Raises Eyebrows with 'Bad Hombres' Line," *Time*, October 19, 2016.

15. Bob Ortega and Rob O'Dell, "Deadly Border Agent Incidents Cloaked in Silence," *The Arizona Republic*, December 16, 2013.

16. Michael D. Shear and Julie Hirschfeld Davis, "Shoot Migrants' Legs, Build Alligator Moat: Behind Trump's Ideas for Border," *The New York Times*, October 1, 2019.

17. Chris Edelson, "Ordinary Americans Carried Out Inhumane Acts for Trump," *The Baltimore Sun*, February 6, 2017.

18. The Marquis de Sade, "Philosophy in the Bedroom," in *Three Complete Novels: Justine, Philosophy in the Bedroom, Eugénie de Franval,*

and Other Writings, ed. and trans. Richard Seaver and Austryn Wainhouse (1782; New York: Grove Press, 1965), 280.

19. Mary Daly, *Beyond God the Father: Toward a Philosophy of Women's Liberation* (Boston: Beacon, 1973), 19.

20. Marta Marchlewska, Aleksandra Cichocka, et al., "Populism as Identity Politics: Perceived In-Group Disadvantage, Collective Narcissism, and Support for Populism," *Social Psychological and Personality Science* 9, no. 2 (March 1, 2018): 151–62.

21. Rebecca Shabad, "Donald Trump Names His Favorite Bible Verse," CBS News, April 14, 2016.

22. Fox News Insider, "Trump Warns GOPers: 'Anybody Who Hits Me, We're Gonna Hit 10 Times Harder,'" *Hannity*, November 3, 2015.

23. "Trump Friend's Company Gets $50 Million Contract," *The New York Times*, April 5, 2020.

24. Charlie Savage, "Trump Suggests He Can Gag Inspector General for Stimulus Bailout Program," *The New York Times*, March 27, 2020.

25. Stephanie Sarkis, "Trump Resorts to Invective at Tulsa Rally," *Forbes*, June 22, 2020.

26. Sarkis, "Trump Resorts to Invective."

27. Geoffrey T. Wodtke, "Are Smart People Less Racist? Verbal Ability, Anti-Black Prejudice, and the Principle-Policy Paradox," *Social Problems* 63, no. 1 (February 2016): 21–45.

28. Robin DiAngelo, "White Fragility," *International Journal of Critical Pedagogy* 3, no. 3 (2011): 64.

Chapter 4

1. *Histories of Herodotus* 1.86.2.

2. Adam Gabbatt, "'Unparalleled Privilege': Why White Evangelicals See Trump as Their Savior," *The Guardian*, January 11, 2020.

3. James S. Gordon, "Does the 'Cyrus Prophecy' Help Explain Evangelical Support for Donald Trump?," *The Guardian*, March 23, 2017.

4. Gabbatt, "'Unparalleled Privilege.'"

5. Daniel Block, "Is Trump Our Cyrus? The Old Testament Case for Yes and No," *Christianity Today*, October 29, 2018.

6. George M. Marsden, *Fundamentalism and American Culture: The Shaping of Twentieth-Century Evangelicalism, 1870–1925* (New York: Oxford University Press, 1980), 48–55.

7. Hal Lindsey, *The Late Great Planet Earth* (Grand Rapids: Zondervan, 1970), 43.

8. Hal Lindsey, *The 1980's: Countdown to Armageddon* (New York: Bantam Books, 1981), 8.

9. Lindsey, *The Late Great Planet Earth*, 95.

10. Mary Clare Jalonick and Matthew Daly, "Trump Says US Will Be Safer, Richer If He Is President," Associated Press, July 22, 2016.

11. Tom Pyszczynski et al., "Mortality Salience, Martyrdom, and Military Might: The Great Satan versus the Axis of Evil," *Personality and Social Psychology Bulletin* 32, no. 4 (May 2006): 525–37.

12. Lindsey, *The Late Great Planet Earth*, 87.

13. "Tracking an Outbreak," *The New York Times*, July 3, 2020.

14. Lindsey, *The Late Great Planet Earth*, 97.

15. Jacob Bogage, "Whom Are You Voting For? This Guy Can Read Your Mind," *The Washington Post*, June 23, 2016.

16. PRRI Staff, "White Evangelical Protestant Attitudes toward Donald Trump, 2015–2019," Public Religion Research Institute, January 3, 2020.

17. Mark Galli, "Trump Should Be Removed from Office: It's Time to Say What We Said 20 Years Ago When a President's Character Was Revealed for What It Was," *Christianity Today*, December 19, 2019.

18. John Grano and Richard Land, "*Christianity Today* and the Problem with 'Christian Elitism,'" *The Christian Post*, December 23, 2019.

19. Lindsey, *The Late Great Planet Earth*, 60.

20. Maegan Vazquez and Allie Malloy, "Trump Says He Spoke with Putin about 'Russian Hoax,' Didn't Warn Him against 2020 Election Meddling," CNN, May 4, 2019.

21. Jake Tapper and Jim Acosta, "'Like Pulling Teeth' to Get White House to Focus on Russian Election Interference, Official Says," CNN, April 24, 2019.

22. Julian E. Barnes and Adam Goldman, "Russia Trying to Incite Racial Violence, Experts Say," *The New York Times*, March 11, 2020.

23. Mujib Mashal, Eric Schmitt, Najim Rahim, and Rukmini Callimachi, "Afghan Contractor Handed Out Russian Cash to Kill Americans, Officials Say," *The New York Times*, July 1, 2020.

24. Richard Luscombe, "'He Was Sent to Us': At Church Rally, Evangelicals Worship God and Trump," *The Guardian*, January 4, 2020. Cf. Lindsey, *The Late Great Planet Earth*, 98–100.

25. Sarah Pulliam Bailey, "'I Am the Chosen One': Trump Again Plays on Messianic Claims as He Embraces 'King of Israel' Title," *The Washington Post*, August 21, 2019.

26. Sean Rossman, "Pompeo Says It's 'Possible' President Trump Raised to 'Save the Jewish People,'" *USA Today*, March 22, 2019.

27. Elizabeth Dias and Jeremy W. Peters, "Evangelical Leaders Close Ranks with Trump after Scathing Editorial," *The New York Times*, December 20, 2019.

28. Andrew Restuccia, "The Sanctification of Donald Trump," *Politico*, April 30, 2019.

29. Aaron Blake, "Trump's Impeachment Is Like Jesus' Crucifixion, the Salem Witch Trials and Pearl Harbor All Rolled into One," *The Washington Post*, December 18, 2019.

30. Eugene Scott, "Trump Believes in God, but Hasn't Sought Forgiveness," CNN, July 18, 2015.

31. Christopher Flavelle et al., "Chief of NOAA Defends Scientists, and President," *The New York Times*, September 11, 2019.

32. Lindsey, *The Late Great Planet Earth*, 96–97.

33. Christina Zhao, "Pastor Says God Will Protect U.S. from Coronavirus because Trump Administration Sided with 'Life in the Womb,'" *Newsweek*, February 16, 2020.

34. Bianca Padró Ocasio, "'Demonic Spirit': Miami Pastor Rejects Coronavirus Warning," *Miami Herald*, March 15, 2020.

35. Ralph Drollinger, "Is God Judging America Today?," *Capitol Ministries*, March 21, 2020, https://capmin.org/is-god-judging-america-today/.

36. Brooke Sopelsa, "Trump Cabinet's Bible Teacher Says Gays among Those to Blame for COVID-19," NBC News, March 25, 2020.

37. Chris Cillizza, "Donald Trump's Appalling, Blame-Shifting Rose Garden News Conference," CNN, March 13, 2020.

38. David Brennan, "China State Media Says Trump Is 'Pandering' to Racists, Pandemic Response Is 'Sloppy and Belated,'" *Newsweek*, March 18, 2010.

39. Shane Harris et al., "U.S. Intelligence Reports from January and February Warned about a Likely Pandemic," *The Washington Post*, March 20, 2020.

40. Jack Kelly, "Senators Accused of Insider Trading, Dumping Stocks after Coronavirus Briefings," *Forbes*, March 20, 2020.

41. Aaron Blake, "A Timeline of Trump Playing Down the Coronavirus Threat," *The Washington Post*, March 17, 2020; Daniel Dale and Tara Subramaniam, "Fact Check: A List of Twenty-Eight Ways Trump and His Team Have Been Dishonest about the Coronavirus," CNN, March 11, 2020.

42. Blake, "A Timeline of Trump Playing Down the Coronavirus Threat."

43. Blake, "A Timeline of Trump Playing Down the Coronavirus Threat."

44. Isabel Togoh, "Texas Official Suggests 'Lots' of Grandparents Would Willing Risk Coronavirus Death to Keep Economy Going," *Forbes*, March 24, 2020.

45. Eric Lipton, Zolan Kanno-Youngs, and Helene Cooper, "Trump Slowly Enlisting More Agencies in 'Whole of Government' Response to Virus," *The New York Times*, March 17, 2020.

46. Blake, "A Timeline of Trump Playing Down the Coronavirus Threat."

47. Lindsey, *The Late Great Planet Earth*, 101.

48. Jason Lemon, "Bush Ethics Lawyer Suggests Trump's Spiritual Advisor Paula White Committing 'Fraud,' and Running a 'Ponzi Scheme,'" *Newsweek*, November 13, 2019.

49. Patricia Mazzei, "Falwells Settle Court Case over Florida Business Deal," *The New York Times*, October 8, 2019.

50. Frances Robles and Jim Rutenberg, "The Evangelical, the 'Pool Boy,' the Comedian, and Michael Cohen," *The New York Times*, June 18, 2019.

51. Brandon Ambrosino, "My Weekend at the Falwells' South Beach Flophouse," *Politico Magazine*, August 25, 2017.

52. Cheryl K. Chumley, "Franklin Graham Blasts Pepsi, NFL for 'Sexual Exploitation,'" *The Washington Times*, February 3, 2020.

53. Yonat Shimron, "Franklin Graham on Impeachment: 'Our Country Could Begin to Unravel,'" *Religion News Service*, October 2, 2019.

54. Lindsey, *The Late Great Planet Earth*, 111.

55. Lindsey, *The Late Great Planet Earth*, 111–19.

56. Lindsey, *The Late Great Planet Earth*, 119.

57. Matthew Haag, "Robert Jeffress, Pastor Who Said Jews Going to Hell, Led Prayer at Jerusalem Embassy," *The New York Times*, May 14, 2018.

58. Haag, "Robert Jeffress."

59. Lindsey, *The Late Great Planet Earth*, 45–46.

60. Richard M. Stana, *INS' Southwest Border Strategy: Resource and Impact Issues Remain after Seven Years* (Washington, DC: US General Accounting Office, 2001), 1.

Chapter 5

1. Katie Rogers, "Watchdog Bares Emails of Trump Aide Pushing White Nationalist Views," *The New York Times*, November 11, 2019.

2. Derek Thompson, "The GOP Needs an Economic Plan for More Than the 'White Establishment,'" *The Atlantic*, November 7, 2012.

3. Barry J. Balleck, ed., "The Turner Diary," in *Modern American Extremism and Domestic Terrorism: An Encyclopedia of Extremists and Extremists Groups* (Santa Barbara, CA: ABC-CLIO, 2018), 369.

4. Linley Sanders, "Charles Manson Is Dead: What Was His 'Helter Skelter' Race War Plan?," *Newsweek*, November 20, 2017.

5. Janell Ross, "Dylann Roof Reportedly Wanted a Race War. How Many Americans Sympathize?," *The Washington Post*, June 19, 2015.

6. Tim Arango, Nicholas Bogel-Burroughs, and Katie Benner, "Minutes Before El Paso Killing, Hate-Filled Manifesto Appears Online," *The New York Times*, August 3, 2019.

7. Erin Donaghue, "Racially-Motivated Violent Extremists Elevated to 'National Threat Priority,' FBI Director Says," CBS News, February 5, 2020.

8. Jeremy W. Peters et al., "How the El Paso Gunman Echoed the Words of Right-Wing Pundits," *The New York Times*, August 12, 2019.

9. Max Rose and Ali H. Soufan, "The White Supremacist Threat Is Real," *The New York Times*, February 12, 2020.

10. Leah Asmelash and Sheena Jones, "New Jersey Just Raised Its Threat Level for White Supremacists to 'High,' Well Above ISIS and Al Qaeda," CNN, February 22, 2020.

11. Josh Margolin, "White Supremacists Encouraging Members to Spread Coronavirus to Cops, Jews: FBI," ABC News, March 22, 2020.

12. Michael Colborne, "As World Struggles to Stop Deaths, Far Right Celebrates COVID-19," *AlJazeera News*, March 26, 2020.

13. Nathan Taylor Pemberton, "What Do You Do When Extremism Comes for the Hawaiian Shirt?," *The New York Times*, June 29, 2020.

14. Craig Timberg, Elizabeth Dwoskin, and Souad Mekhennet, "Men Wearing Hawaiian Shirts and Carrying Guns Add a Volatile New Element to Protests," *The Washington Post*, June 4, 2020.

15. Katelyn Newberg, "3 Alleged 'Boogaloo' Members Charged in Las Vegas Protests," *Las Vegas Review-Journal*, June 3, 2020.

16. Neil MacFarquhar, Alan Feuer, and Adam Goldman, "Police Dismiss Trump's Claim of Antifa Plots," *The New York Times*, June 12, 2020.

17. Lawrence Hurley, "Trump Coronavirus Guidance on Keeping Gun Stores Open Draws Criticism," *Reuters*, March 30, 2020.

18. Neil MacFarquhar, "Company Redirects Online Searches for Hate Material to Ads with a Very Different Message," *The New York Times*, December 31, 2019.

19. Colborne, "As World Struggles."

20. "CSPI Urges FDA Enforcement Action on Televangelist Jim Bakker's Fake Coronavirus 'Cure,'" Center for Science in the Public Interest, February 20, 2020.

21. Leonard Blair, "Paula White: Christians Will 'Stand Accountable before God' If They Vote against Trump," *The Christian Post*, October 24, 2019.

22. Robert Jeffress, *Fox and Friends Weekend*, September 29, 2019.

23. Yonat Shimron, "Franklin Graham on Impeachment: 'Our Country Could Begin to Unravel,'" *Religion News Service*, October 2, 2019.

24. Reis Thebault, "News Outlet That Covered 'Lizard People' and Called Obama a Demon Just Interviewed Trump Jr.," *The Washington Post*, March 29, 2019.

25. Rick Wiles, *TruNews*, https://www.youtube.com/watch?v=ENId FPhivHY&feature=youtu.be.

26. US Equal Employment Opportunity Commission, "Fact Sheet: Immigrants' Employment Rights under Federal Anti-Discrimination Laws," April 27, 2010.

27. Sara Sidner, "Tracking the Disturbing Rise of White Supremacist Propaganda," CNN, February 15, 2020.

28. "Fractured Nation: Widening Partisan Polarization and Key Issues in 2020 Presidential Elections," Public Religion Research Institute, October 20, 2019.

29. "Fractured Nation."

30. David Nakamura, Ashley Parker, Colby Itkowitz, and Maria Sacchetti, "At Mount Rushmore, Trump Exploits Social Divisions, Warns of 'Left-Wing Cultural Revolution' in Dark Speech Ahead of Independence Day," *The Washington Post*, July 3, 2020.

31. Rogers, "Watchdog Bares E-mails."

32. Adeel Hassan, "Assaults Linked to Hate Crimes Were Up in 2008 According to F. B. I.," *The New York Times*, November 13, 2019.

33. David Brennan, "China State Media Says Trump Is 'Pandering' to Racists, Pandemic Response Is 'Sloppy and Belated,'" *Newsweek*, March 18, 2010.

34. Cynthia Silva, "US Veterans Volunteer to Patrol SF Chinatown amid Coronavirus-Related Racism," NBC News, March 30, 2020.

35. Grace Panetta, "Twitter Reportedly Won't Use an Algorithm to Crack Down on White Supremacists Because Some GOP Politicians Could End Up Getting Barred Too," *Business Insider*, April 25, 2019.

36. Roberto S. Goizueta, *Caminemos con Jesús: Toward a Hispanic/Latino Theology of Accompaniment* (Maryknoll, NY: Orbis Books, 1995), 192.

37. "Coronavirus: Sikh Volunteers Prepare Over 30,000 Meals Packets for Americans in Self-Isolation," *Asian News International*, March 24, 2020.

38. Miriam Rizk, "Egypt Fears New Coptic Christmas Eve Attack," Associated Press, January 6, 2013.

39. Miguel A. De La Torre, *The Immigration Crisis: Toward an Ethics of Place* (Eugene, OR: Cascade Books, 2016), 109–30.

40. Jürgen Moltmann, *Theology of Hope: On the Ground and the Implications of a Christian Eschatology*, trans. James W. Leitch (New York: Harper & Row, 1967), 20–25.

41. Miguel A. De La Torre, *Liberating Jonah: Forming an Ethics of Reconciliation* (Maryknoll, NY: Orbis Books, 2007), 142–47.

42. Miguel A. De La Torre, *Latina/o Social Ethics: Moving Beyond Eurocentric Moral Thinking* (Waco, TX: Baylor University Press, 2010), 92–93.

43. Sam Dorman, "Clarence Thomas Reportedly Compares 'The Modern-Day Liberal' to Klansmen in New Doc," Fox News, November 30, 2020.

44. Aaron E. Sanchez, "Who Are the Latino Evangelicals That Support Trump?," *Sojourners*, November 26, 2019.

45. "Fractured Nation."

46. Mark Oppenheimer, "A Theologian's Influence and Stained Past Live On," *The New York Times*, October 11, 2013.

47. Frederick John Dalton, *The Moral Vision of César Chávez* (Maryknoll, NY: Orbis Books, 2003), 143.

48. Sarah Wheaton and Michael D. Shear, "Blunt Report Says G. O. P. Needs to Regroup for '16," *The New York Times*, March 18, 2013.